W9-AVM-053

50+ Vacation Homes

50 +Vacation Homes

Edited by Andrea Boekel

images
Publishing

Published in Australia in 2006 by
The Images Publishing Group Pty Ltd
ABN 89 059 734 431
6 Bastow Place, Mulgrave, Victoria 3170, Australia
Tel: +61 3 9561 5544 Fax: +61 3 9561 4860
books@images.com.au
www.imagespublishing.com

Copyright © The Images Publishing Group Pty Ltd 2006
The Images Publishing Group Reference Number: 674

All rights reserved. Apart from any fair dealing for the purposes of
private study, research, criticism or review as permitted under the
Copyright Act, no part of this publication may be reproduced,
stored in a retrieval system or transmitted in any form by any
means, electronic, mechanical, photocopying, recording or
otherwise, without the written permission of the publisher.

National Library of Australia Cataloguing-in-Publication entry:
50+ Vacation Homes.
Includes index.

ISBN 1 92074 499 1.

1. 50+ Vacation homes. 2. Vacation homes – Designs and plans
3. Architecture, Domestic. I. Boekel, Andrea
728.7

Edited by Andrea Boekel

Designed by The Graphic Image Studio Pty Ltd, Mulgrave, Australia
www.tgis.com.au

Digital production by Splitting Image Colour Studio Pty Ltd
Printed by Everbest Printing Co. Ltd., in Hong Kong/China

IMAGES has included on its website a page for special notices in
relation to this and our other publications. Please visit
www.imagespublishing.com

Contents

Introduction

The vacation home will always hold infinite appeal to most because it embodies a consciousness of a very significant need: the need for retreat, leisure and recreation. The desire to rejuvenate spirit and body is inherent in all of us and nowhere is this need more fulfilled than in a vacation spot.

Vacation homes are the manifestation of those who have been able to realise the universal dream of creating exclusive hideaways. The projects featured are portrayals of homes to 'get away from it all' and span many diverse locations in different countries in settings that are just as varied. From valleys shielded by forbidding, craggy peaks, to the sparse beauty of the ochre and russet desert landscape; from alpine nooks shrouded in cloaks of snow to cliff tops that straddle the dazzling blue waters of the ocean; the beautiful residences within the pages of *50+ Vacation Homes* are demonstrations of homeowners' visions translated into architectural ingenuity. The emphasis throughout the book is on residences that complement the terrain; not smother it.

The Aarthun Residence in Palm Desert, California that embraces the desert landscape into its very core; the Villa Bled in Gorenjska, Slovenia, on the banks of a lovely alpine lake; the House in Mani in Greece nestling in an olive grove that typifies the Mediterranean villa with its stuccoed walls; the Nature House outside São Paulo, Brazil that utilises the bounty of nature in its building scheme with wood, sisal, and burnt cement and the House in Régua, entrenched in the romantic lore of the port-wine producing vineyard region of Portugal; these extraordinary houses fit into their site, lift out the decisive views, and pay heed to nature and place.

50+ Vacation Homes presents residences from Europe, North and South America, the Far East and Australasia and offers insights into signature homes geared for rest and recreation. Vivid and stunning photography brings the houses and their surroundings to life. Detailed descriptions that are not mere mechanical summaries, but evaluations of the needs of both architect and owner, provide a personal peek into the design process that may help build readers' own dreams.

Leisure, recreation, comfort and relaxation are what a vacation home represents and that is the focus of this rare and exceptional compendium. It is a visual journey to many exotic locations: an inspirational and stirring tribute to these gorgeous homes that merge space, light, colour and site to create the perfect getaway.

Andrea Boekel
Editor

Aarthun Residence

The striking architecture of this 565-square-metre house makes it a living sculpture. The site affords views of the Santa Rosa Mountains, the golf course and the breathtaking panorama of the valley.

The weather-toughened, stone-clad face of this desert home is turned to the street, displaying strength and stability. Once past the front gate, a sheltered forecourt appears. From here the house reveals itself gradually, the gate opening into a garden with a stone-paved walkway leading to the main door. The elegant entry foyer is composed of glass panes set between two partially suspended granite slabs.

The other three façades contrast with the front of the building generating a feeling of expansion and introducing bold curves, dramatic use of maintenance-free materials and indigenous landscaping. The entire exterior is composed of stone, copper and glass with the main roof a copper-covered, barrel-vaulted roof sliced in half to allow clerestory glass windows on each side.

1

The living room has views in all directions. Sliding glass doors disappear into pockets in the walls, dissolving the boundary between indoor and out. The dining room also has views both sides. The sit-down sunken bar can be an indoor area when the glass doors are closed or an outdoor area when the doors are open.

The family room opens to the outside with glass doors that slide away out of sight. The master suite uses a wall of glass to capture the panoramic views of mountains and golf course. Attached to the master suite is a home/office retreat. Totally independent, but equally luxurious, the detached guesthouse has all the amenities of the master suite and is considered a second master suite.

Surrounded by a large deck and entertainment patio area, the pool hosts an outcrop of semi-submerged boulders that appear to cascade into it fusing it with the surrounding desert. The view from this area is spectacular. With the environment in mind, sustainable design concepts were adopted in the design. The monolithic type stone columns near the fire serve as thermal mass, a heat energy bank storing heat and releasing it gradually into the surrounding rooms. The slide-away glass walls allow for the entry of cooling breezes.

Throughout the house textures set up contrasts. Highly polished areas abut carpeted regions and meet at rough stone walls. Sunlight enters during the day through windows set close to the ceiling, while tiny star-like lights illuminate during the hours of dark. The entire house conjures up a feeling of 'outside in and the inside out' and encourages 'resort living', a term that implies spending as much time outdoors as indoors.

Patel Architecture/Narendra Patel, AIA

1   Free-flowing and meandering lines of pool are designed as extension to house
2   Exterior is composed of different architectural forms covered with stone, copper and glass
Following pages:
    Pool area with large patio and deck spaces is capable of hosting parties for large groups

4 Dining room separated from entry foyer by suspended granite buffet countertop held up by glass
5 Fireplace with poured-in-place concrete masses encompasses cone-shaped copper container
6 Double-island kitchen opens to family room. Second island is designed for light meals and is also a functional centrepiece
7 Master bedroom
Photography: Nicola Pira

4

6

7

Abreu Family Residence

Guarujá, São Paulo, Brazil

Located in the beachside area of Guarujá, this house is 90 kilometres from São Paulo. It is an area of quiet tranquillity despite being relatively near the city.

A huge 6000 square metres in size, the house overlooks the ocean at the front and the Serro do Mar Mountains at the rear. The prime objective of the design was to take advantage of the beautiful mountain views at the rear of the house as an alternative to the busy, crowded beach at the front.

The client required a comfortable house for his extended family to retreat to on weekends and holidays. The architect, an admirer of the prairie houses of Frank Lloyd Wright and the Brazilian colonial houses of Ouro Preto designed this house to incorporate both concepts. Traditional Brazilian colonial house-style was adopted for the clay-tile roof. Large balconies protect the house from the constant, hot sun and occasional, torrential downpours of rain. Wright's concept was adopted in the interesting use of spaces.

Separate areas for guests and family are linked through a 15-metre bridge over the patio entrance. Throughout the house there are multiple accommodation and social areas, some formal, others more casual. A large classic swimming pool, tennis court, indoor jacuzzi and open kitchen area cater for a range of holiday activities.

One of the aesthetically pleasing features of this house is the square decorative columns dispersed along the covered walkways and indoor/outdoor areas. Strong, exposed, ornate trusses support the painted planked ceiling in the informal social area and open kitchen, while flat ceilings give a more contained feel to the formal areas.

The house is surrounded by beautiful landscaped gardens that face both beach and mountains. The driveway, flanked by palms, presents a dramatic entrance through the large main gates to the house.

Large, spacious and comfortable, the home exudes an air of calm and serenity, wafted through by cooling breezes and warmed by filtered sunlight.

1 Large windows offer views towards beach
Opposite:
   Palm-lined driveway leading to house

1

Opposite:
    View of swimming pool
4   Path alongside house
5   Front garden facing beach
6   Garden pavilion

4

5

6

7

8

10

Opposite:
    Living room with dining area beyond
10   View of kitchen
11   Spa
Photography: Rômulo Fialdini

11

Arraial D'Ajauda

Bahia, Brazil

The artist's impression of this house has been beautifully realised in this home, skilfully marrying contemporary design and the cultural traditions of the region.

The stiff peaks of the roof rise through the air between swaying coconut palms on this beachside site. Wide open verandas present ample opportunity for relaxation, enhanced by the combination of local craftsman-made, simple, rustic furniture especially designed by the architect. Colourful sofas, hammocks and comfortable chairs beckon from under the cool retreat of the eaves which cover the wooden deck and provide a frame for a view of the isolated beach beyond.

The wood-constructed residence is generous in size, and divided into sections for living and sleeping spaces. The towering palms outside are echoed inside by tall beams, bound and carved in the manner of ancient house building. Structural features dominate, complemented by plain non-intrusive walls, offering a harmonious transition between urban life and nature.

A stroll around the site reveals an interesting and surprising use of materials: rock, wood and burnt cement are all used creatively and resourcefully.

Surrounded by colourful gardens where much of the native vegetation has been retained, the house is infused with a sense of tranquillity: enclosed areas seeming to merge with the outside.

The house is a wonderful example of how an exciting design can be translated into a vibrant reality.

1

Fabrizio Ceccarelli Arquiteto

2

3

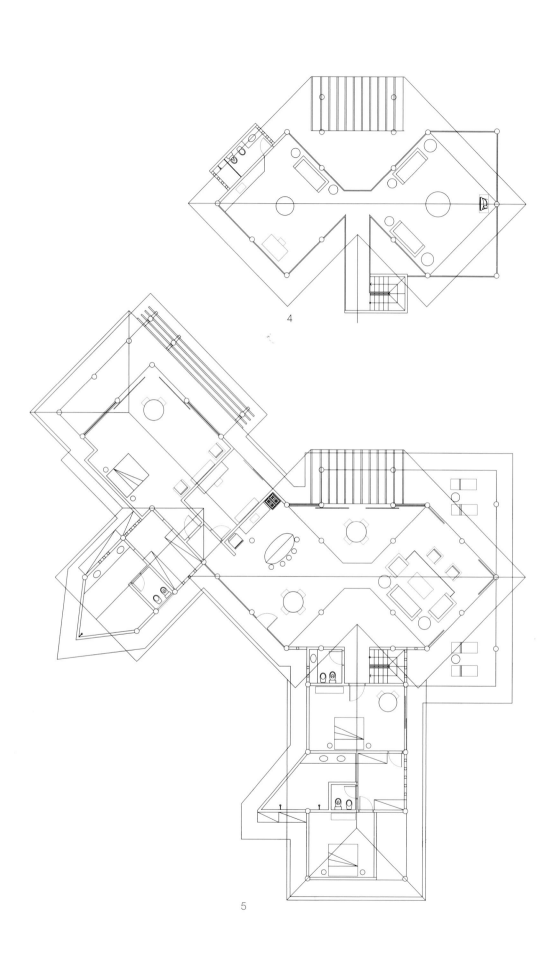

4

5

6

7

9

9 House is set amid coconut palms
10 Outdoor terrace
11 View of golf course
Photography: Gal Oppido

10

11

Baan Hua Hin

Hua Hin, Prachuap Khriri
Khan, Thailand

1

1   Foyer view from main entrance
2   Communal pavilion living room looking towards pool and sea

Hua Hin, a district in Prachaup Khriri Khan, is a two-hour hour drive south
of Bangkok. Popular as a weekend sanctuary for the Thais since King
Rama VII built Wang Klai Kangwon in the early 1900s, it entertains visitors
on its miles of golden sandy beaches. The brief for this residence was to
provide a weekend and vacation retreat for a Thai businessman and his
family to escape from their busy lives in Bangkok.

The site is narrow, and at its longest only 100 metres. Rows of bungalows
and houses face the beach minimising views. Flanked by neighbouring
houses on either side, it has limited visual access. A long decked area
provides a feeling of open space.

The client's initial desire was for a design that reflected the history of
Hua Hin. He also required a house with a variety of easily maintained
internal spaces.

The house is defined by three pavilions stretched over the site to face
the sea. The service, sleeping and communal pavilions are located in
successive order from the street. Courtyards between each pavilion
provide alternative views and leisure spaces, while plants serve to soften
the geometry of the house. Each pavilion has been carefully planned to
fulfill its function: the comfort and enjoyment of its occupants. The skins
of the living and dining rooms, located closest to the beach, have been
designed to be mostly transparent so that nature is embraced as part of
the design. The bedrooms, located in the middle pavilion use untreated
wooden, slatted skin to provide shade and at the same time blend with
the surroundings.

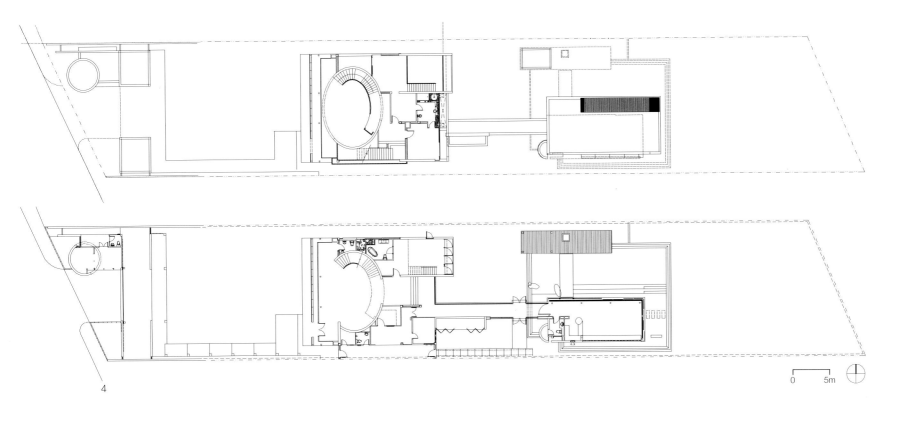

4

0   5m

6

Opposite:
   Master bedroom
4 Second-floor and first-floor plan
5 Private outdoor jacuzzi
6 Main stairs to master bedroom

5

7   Living room in area where bedrooms are located
8&9   Bathroom
Opposite:
       Living room
Photography: Wilson Tungthunya and Architects 49

7

8

9

Baan Patong

This vacation home located in Phuket is built on a steep slope overlooking a bay and the resort city of Patong. The site is thickly vegetated in a region of tall, slender, rubber and coconut trees. The house takes advantage of the site by following the contour of the land and permitting the spaces to have views out to the bay.

Baan Patong is divided into three main areas: a living area, multipurpose and a guest area. Each area is self-contained and fully serviced.

The detailing responds to the tropical climate. Large, overhanging roofs provide ample shade and protection from monsoon rains. The house's open features allow for ventilation from ocean breezes through the use of large, glass-paned windows. A large shaded outdoor terrace permits residents to enjoy natural fresh air rather than remain in air-conditioned areas indoors.

Local materials are used for finishing, including the wood flooring, with teak detailing and local granite walls. The materials used ensure this large house is blended into the hillside. Large boulders from the site are incorporated into the design with the intention of recreating the landscape of the surrounding forest.

1

1   Large roof overhangs are characteristic of this house
Opposite:
    View from pool balcony to main house

3

4

5

6

7

9

Opposite:
  Main stairway
 9 Stairway with terrace and games room
   alongside sunken court
10 Ground-floor plan
11 Main stairway to master bedroom
12 Main kitchen with double-height ceiling
13 Senior family member's bathroom
Following pages:
  Formal living room with large glazed
  areas with views to surrounding nature

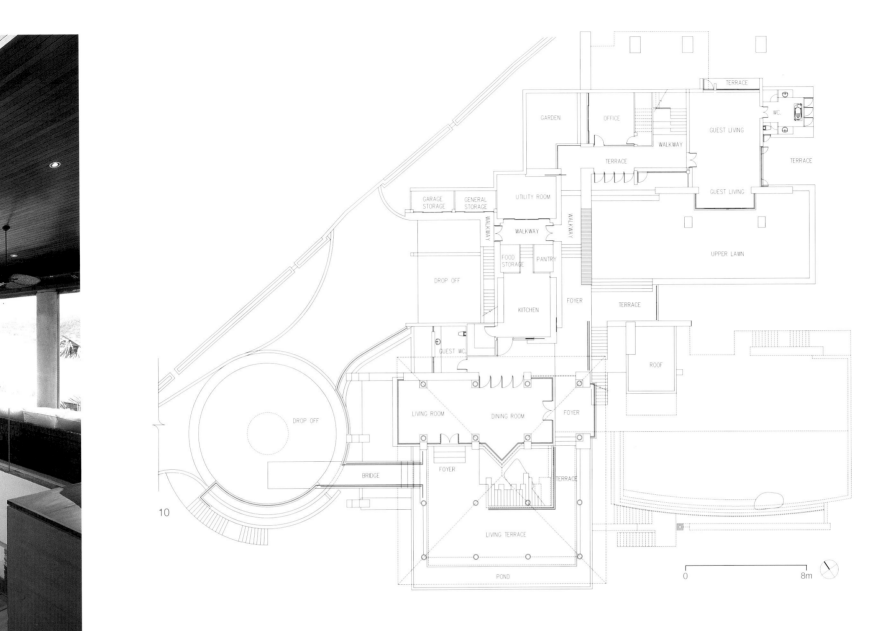

10

11

12

13

15

16

17

15 Dining room
16 Senior family member's bedroom
17 Formal living room
Photography: Wilson Tungthunya

Baan Pattaya

Baan Pattaya (Pattaya House) is a one and two-storey clustered structure vacation home. It is divided into three different utility spaces consisting of main living quarters, children and guest quarters and a service building located separately. The overall design evokes the spirit of the Thai lifestyle.

Sited in an open field atop a hill, the house is hidden deep in a park, within part of an estate called 'The Ocean View Project' (Bang Sa-Re). The location offers magnificent views of Pattaya Bay over the coconut fields.

Each building is located in the most beautiful area of the site, and provides a comfortable environment for living in Thailand's tropical climate, while blending easily with the Thai community.

The design for a contemporary Thai lifestyle is achieved in many ways. Traditional Thai house characteristics have been physically combined with a modern living space and configured to respond to the site surroundings. They have been blended with western standards of comfort. Elements such as posts, beams and braces, from traditional Thai houses are included. The ground floor level is of a design that enables the walls to be opened and closed as desired. Folding doors add security and privacy.

Further embodying the 'Thai spirit', the colours and finishes, such as natural wood reminiscent of traditional Thai houses, add value. Locally sourced finishing materials of wooden lath and clay tiles for the roof are assembled together in clean, contemporary lines emphasising their natural colours and preserving their timeless beauty. A dark-grey tone for other areas of the house ensures the seamless merging of the building with its surrounds.

The landscape features a pond that mimics a winding creek and its ecosystem. The interior design makes a play on this theme creating an atmosphere that is alive and vibrant. The design uses those especially selected finishing materials that are at the core of Thai building and serve to invoke the 'Thai spirit'.

1   Breakfast nook
Opposite:
    View of main entrance

1

4

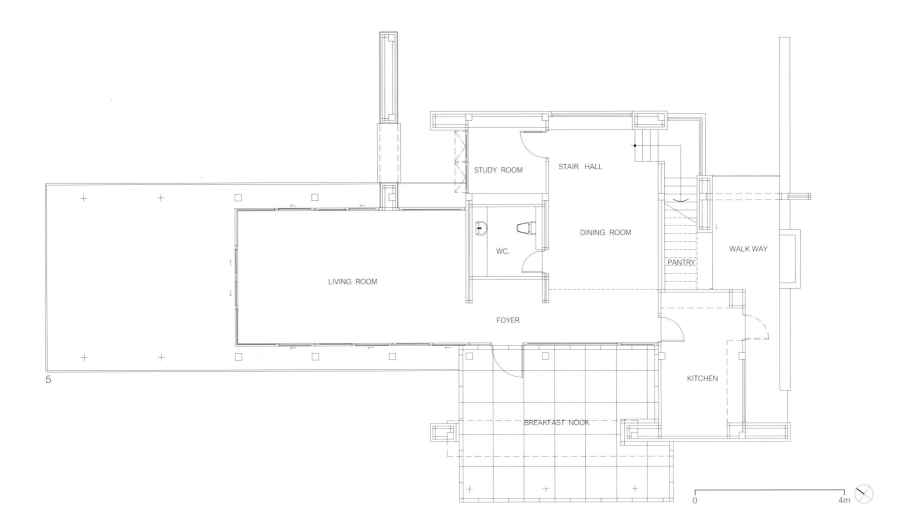

STUDY ROOM
STAIR HALL
DINING ROOM
WC.
WALK WAY
PANTRY
LIVING ROOM
FOYER
KITCHEN
BREAKFAST NOOK

5

0 4m

6

7

8

5 First-floor plan of main house
6 Second-floor master bedroom patio
7 Living room with panoramic views
8 Master bedroom with folded window

9　Master bathroom blends traditional
　　Thai and contemporary styles
10　Master bedroom with semi-outdoor
　　jacuzzi
Opposite:
　　Dining room
Photography: Wilson Tungthunya
and Architects 49

9

10

The Ballerina House

Rancho Mirage, California, USA

The design of The Ballerina House was inspired in part by the fluidity in the movements of ballet. The architect's wife is a ballet dancer and choreographer. The house was meant to be experimental and many artists collaborated with the architect to experiment with new ideas, materials, techniques, forms and surfaces. Art and architecture were therefore seamlessly blended together.

Mapped human movements of choreography were used to produce images of pure digital data and translated into graphic lines, which were used throughout the house. Fluid, dimensionless architecture was thus combined with strong geometry to create intriguing spaces.

The exposed concrete floor was engraved with flowing lines that were also derived from digitally tracking the movements of the ballet dancer. Natural shapes abound throughout the house. The entry door design was derived from Da Vinci's study of a nautilus shell. A granite fireplace in the living room echoes the surrounding mountains outside. The chandelier in the dining room is made of a stainless steel cable structure combined with conceptual hand-drawn sketches of the house at the design stage. The entry gate conveys a sense of 'celebration of arrival' in a symphony of copper and bronze.

The pool serves as a centrepiece, creating an inside/outside space. The free-flowing and meandering lines of the pool were designed to be consistent with the overall ballet theme of the house.

1

Patel Architecture/Narendra Patel, AIA

1   Entry gate
2   Free-flowing and meandering lines of pool
    were designed to follow ballet theme

3 Entry door design was derived from Da Vinci's study of nautilus shell
4 Meandering lines on exposed concrete floor, ceiling and hand-painted fabric on the chair were
  derived from digitally tracking the movements of the ballet dancer
5 Granite fireplace in great room echoes profiles of surrounding mountains

3

4

5

6 Kitchen with insulated skylight in centre for natural light
7 Chandelier in dining room is of stainless steel cable structure combined with conceptual hand-drawn sketches of house
8 Pool serves as focal point with house wrapped around it

6

7

8

9   Master bedroom
10   Master bath with large picture window looking over
     at bath garden and wall mural outside
Photography: Nicola Pira

10

Bayside Residence

This 190-square-metre home is located on a coastal bluff overlooking Cape Cod Bay. The house runs along the top of a ridge and is intended to harmonise with the environment. The design developed as a trapezoidal footprint with two wings separated by a dramatic entrance hallway. The design expresses the functional separation of living and sleeping spaces.

The living wing has been rotated to align with views of the sunset, the bay and Provincetown. The central space on this side of the house contains a large, communal living area that features soaring full-height windows, as well as a dining area, sitting area and a galley kitchen that leads to a screened porch.

The smaller-scale bedrooms are nestled in the opposite wing of the home. The bedroom wing is located parallel to the edge of the property to better utilise the contours of the land and facilitate entry. Much of the home's allure derives from its use of alcoves and nooks as counterpoints to expansive shared spaces.

The wide central staircase is constructed at an angle that mimics the sloping outdoor terrain surrounding the house. An inviting second-storey loft offers privacy but looks down over the open living and dining areas. The loft and an outdoor deck share a sweeping bay view that extends north to Provincetown.

Windows are carefully placed to introduce natural light, capture prevailing southwest breezes and provide natural ventilation. These windows are shielded from rain and sun by the broad overhanging roof.

1   Deck above screened porch
2   Exterior of bayside façade looking east
3   Interior view of kitchen
4   Interior view of living/dining room
Photography: Mark D. Hammer

Hammer Architects

2

3

4

Bernstein House

Long Island, New York, USA

Designed as a weekend retreat for a family of four, the appearance of this house is of a simple French farmhouse. The clients wanted a stucco residence of a minimum of 465 square metres to meet a property requirement. At first glance, the house has many features common to a traditional French country residence with French doors and shuttered windows. Inside, however, the interior is modern and flooded with openness and light.

The house was to be set more than halfway back on its long, two-acre lot offering a sense of grandeur on approach. It was to have a symmetrical entry façade, and to be elegant but simple in its finishes.

An arched gateway leads, between shuttered French doors, to a widening outdoor hallway, front door and paved court beyond. The main part of the house forms an L-shape around the paved courtyard and swimming pool. The third wall of the courtyard is created by the guesthouse and trellis, facing out toward the back lawn.

The glass front door opens into a two storey hall with light from upper storey windows and multiple French doors illuminating the staircase and opening onto the courtyard. The lower hall leads past an open dining room to a grand living room with a huge studio window facing the garden. The floor throughout is honed Portuguese grey limestone. Walls of smooth plaster contrast with painted wood boards above exposed beams in the ceiling. The owners have an eclectic collection of art and the light and expansive wall spaces provide perfect settings for their larger paintings.

The kitchen is in the southeast corner of the house to capture morning light. Bead-board cabinetry and a window seat for the breakfast table gives a cosy relaxed feel. The centre island and counters are covered in beige 'Gascoigne Blue' granite.

The staircase and balcony overlooking the main hall divide the second floor into wings. On one side is the master bedroom suite, whilst the other side leads to an office, two children's bedrooms, bathrooms and a small laundry. The end of this area becomes a sitting nook with a television. Below this wing, to the far side of the outdoor entry area, is a guest bedroom and beyond that a garage. A recreation room and mechanical spaces lie beneath the living room, dining room and kitchen area.

This house is designed to age well and its classic appearance will keep it from dating. Materials throughout were carefully chosen for their refinement and durability. While the house is modern in its detail, it will gracefully age and mature, accepting wear and patina.

1

3 Entrance to courtyard
4 First-floor plan
5 Pool terrace
6 Breakfast table

3

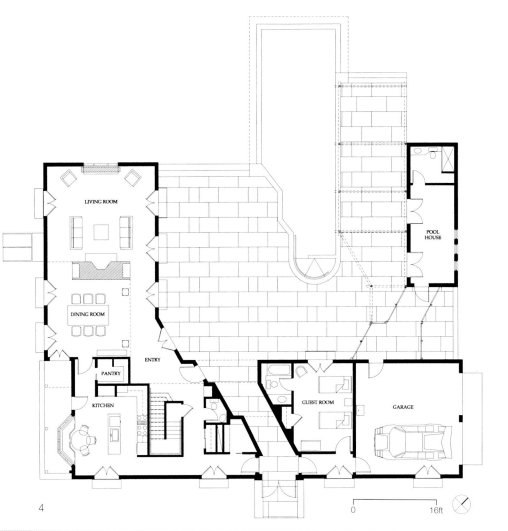

4

POOL HOUSE

LIVING ROOM

DINING ROOM

ENTRY

PANTRY

KITCHEN

GUEST ROOM

GARAGE

0   16ft

5

7

7 Two-storey entrance hall
8 Living room
Opposite:
    Living room with studio window overlooking garden
Photography: Jeff Goldberg/Esto Photographics

8

Country House in Campos do Jordão

São Paulo, Brazil

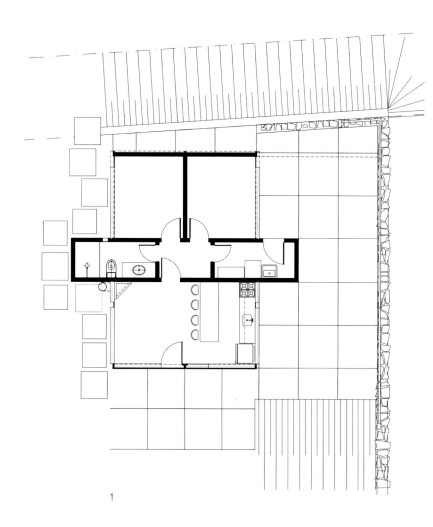

1

This small, country-style house in metropolitan São Paulo reflects a recent unusual demand in Brazil for small scale dwellings. Located in Campos do Jordão, it was completed as a solid structure despite its limited budget.

The architect designed a 50-square-metre unit with two bedrooms, a bathroom, living room and kitchen. An additional laundry can be converted into a second bathroom if required.

The somewhat experimental construction technique has a metallic structure, with pillars and trusses re-covered by metal sheeting. These have been welded together to form a unique surface.

The project can be easily assembled onsite using prefabricated components and finished with metal, bricks and tiles.

Carlos Bratke Ateliê de Arquitetura S/C Ltda

1 Floor plan
2 View of house
3 View from garden with detail of framed roof
4 Front view
5 Living room with fireplace
Photography: Caca Bratke

Encinos Residence

Bosques de las Lomas,
Mexico City, Mexico

The design intention of this project was to create a refined and elegant space while retaining a casual and informal atmosphere. To achieve this objective, classical style was distorted to create spatial qualities through the use of interesting materials: Indian granite, stone from Huixquilucan and American cherry wood.

Classicism interpreted in contemporary fashion is a singular feature of this house. Stone exteriors suggest a Mediterranean villa and create a rustic yet modern image. The main façade presents a covered portico that intersects the tube-like access, conveying the outside inside and vice versa. The use of granite on floors and walls blend with the interior.

The building is constructed on three levels. The highest level contains three bedrooms, bathrooms and a lounge. Skilful blending of artificial and natural light sources emphasises the beauty of the materials used.

The main lobby, living and dining room, toilet and kitchen are located on the second level. Large windows with distinguishing arcs add a measure of formality, affording panoramic views of the vistas towards the ravine beyond.

The recreation room, cellar and garage are located on the first floor. Use of quarry and river stone in these areas add interest.

The high altitude of the site facilitates views of the exceptionally beautiful and dramatic surroundings.

1   Covered portico provides access to garden via classical arches of Indian sandstone
Opposite:
   Indian sandstone complements classical feel of three-level abode

1

Carlos Pascal Arquitectos

3

4

3 Large, spacious living area
4 Raised dining area
5 Cosy accents such as fireplaces add feeling of warmth

6

7

8

9

6 Bedroom
7 Interior with stairway beyond
8 Bathroom
9 Stairway landing
10 Bedroom spaces are generous and offer comfort and elegance
Photography: Victor Benitez

EOS – Mexico's Diamond

Acapulco, Guerrero, Mexico

An unsurpassed frame with the union of infinite blue sky and sea, EOS is an exclusive development in Punta Diamante. With spectacular views of new Acapulco, it is strategically located near the international airport, Del Sol highway, Punta Diamente's marina and the spectacular bay for which this popular tourist location is famed.

EOS was designed as two apartment buildings, five and six levels respectively. Each apartment has two levels to capture the magnificent surrounding views.

1

An important design challenge was the terrain's descending slope. The slab of the highest apartment is used as parking space. This space is located at sidewalk level and from here the apartments develop downwards. Access to the apartments is via a network of ramps and bridges connected to the stairs and elevator at the central 'core' of the building. This area is located at the main access.

Transparency is the keyword: all spaces are in total harmony with the light throughout the day. Indirect illumination at night accentuates the spaces with ethereal reflections and shadows while the magnificent view over the surroundings adds to the allure.

The white walls, visible concrete, steel, aluminium, transparent and burnished glass, marble floors and wood, blends interior and exterior spaces. Natural materials are integrated with water and light so that every detail helps to emphasise the space and offer an innovative design model.

The development's architectural ingenuity begins from the exterior. To avoid direct sunlight, side walls with openings complement a crystal and wooden blind and double-height façade. Not only is this visually attractive but it also serves a practical purpose.

Amenities such as the gymnasium, tennis court, spa, mini-golf course and outdoor bar are connected directly to the swimming pool. The swimming pool is a focal attraction in the building's perception because all other spaces converge there. This concept makes a direct connection with the outdoors. View, nature and landscape; embodying the spirit of Acapulco, EOS provides the ultimate in physical and mental relaxation.

Daniel Pérez Gil Arquitectos

3 Sail over swimming pool deck
4 View from swimming pool
5 Swimming pool and deck
6 Path leading to swimming pool

3

4

5

7 View from living room to terrace
8 View from apartment entrance
9 Master bedroom
10 View from terrace
Photography: Hector Armando Herrera

7

8

9

10

Frye Residence

San Miguel de Allende, Mexico

The renovation of this once nondescript dwelling has transformed the building into a spacious, 300-square-metre contemporary vacation home. The home is sited within the beautiful 460-year-old Mexican colonial town of San Miguel de Allende. It had been designed to optimise the capture of natural light, and uses bold colours, a rich palette of materials, thick walls, curves, straight and rectangular shapes to create a place of dramatic contrasts. The original 116-square-metre, two-storey home was sited on a 7.5 x 18-metre lot and consisted of traditional small rooms with low ceilings. After living in the home for a few years, the owner acquired a similar-sized adjacent lot, in order to enlarge and open up his retreat.

From the street, a rugged stone wall and a deeply-set door of thick pine timber laced into a powerful wooden grid – serves to both invite and protect this home. From inside the entry door, a 4.5-metre-tall glass grid gives visual access through a garden into the living room: strong in colour and form. Another grid of glass opposite opens to a rear garden with a small orchard of citrus trees. The brick-domed 'boveda' ceiling soars to 5.5 metres capping the living room. A sense of openness is created by the long, concrete fireplace hearth, deep-set niches and floor-to-ceiling glass. Looking out into gardens the kitchen links both parts of the house, opening with a bar counter to the living room and through an art niche to the dining room. Hand-made pine cabinets are aniline-dyed to a deep, burgundy colour. Steel-trowelled concrete counters and nook seating is burnished smooth in a rich ochre colour.

The quiet, private master suite on the upper floor has terraces each side inviting sun and providing views in every direction. The bedroom is also capped with a brick-domed 'boveda' ceiling, and the thick walls are sculpted into deep windowsills and a headboard. A two-sided fireplace links the bedroom with the hand-sculpted soaking tub – burnished in wine-coloured concrete – that wraps into the fireplace and forms deep sills and ledges. The entire bath and entry/stair area of the master suite is topped with a brick barrel vault that spans above walls, visually enlarging the space. A multicoloured tile mural, beginning at the shower, covers the wall and floor and spills into the bottom of the tub. Glass blocks are individually set and grouped into thick walls to offer privacy and reflect sparkles of light as the sun moves through the days and seasons.

Mexican tile flooring has been stained a deep rose and scattered with decorative, deep-purple accent tiles. Integrally coloured concrete in ochre and burgundy are burnished smooth and their natural mottling gives a warm touch to the counters, columns, benches and sinks. Inspired by the owner's paintings, soft shades of plum and sage green with accents of deep turquoise colour the walls. The effect is to layer the walls and spaces against each other and provide a beautiful background for the owner's art collection.

Opposite:
Living room

2 First-floor plan
3 Second-floor plan
4 Detail of stairway from rear garden
5 Master bedroom with bathroom beyond
Opposite:
    View of living room from entry garden

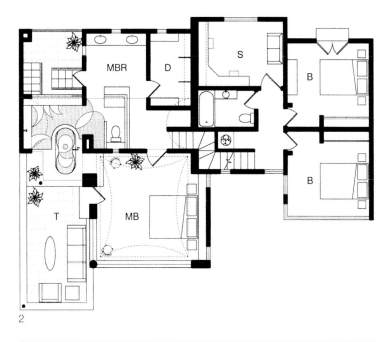

2

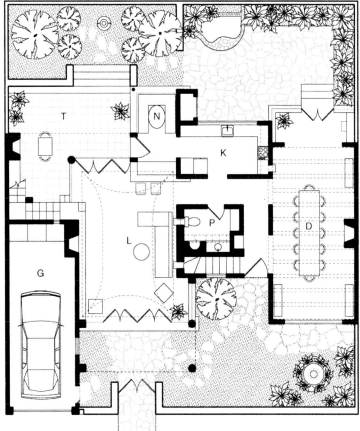

3

4

5

9

8

10

Gallery in Kiyosato

Kiyosato, Yamanashi Prefecture, Japan

Located on the southeast foothills of Mt. Yatsukgatake, 1300 metres above sea level, this site is subject to extremes of cold and dryness. The temperature often drops to –20 degrees Celsius. The site lies within a dense coniferous wooded area, and is 63 metres deep and approximately 17 metres wide. The terrain slopes slightly downward from west to east by four metres, with a stream on the eastern boundary that abuts a protected primeval forest.

Inspired in part by the tall and slender larch trees on the site, the architect was also motivated towards his design by the painting of artist Rene Magritte called *Le Blanc-Seing*. The trees have withstood the harsh winter climate for centuries and his building seems to sit into the landscape as if it belonged there.

The complex use of convex and concave curved walls gives this building a unique, dramatic presence. It was designed as a combination of exhibition space and guesthouse for a client, an executive banker who had lived overseas for many years, who was keen to have 'a house for arts in the forest'. He wanted to be able to share this space with friends, and to display his collections of art and ancient Buddhist sculptures. The layout therefore consists of both primary and secondary spaces. The primary space is open to interpretation, serving a multitude of functions and offering freedom for a variety of activities. The secondary space is a ship-shaped area containing the kitchen, entertainment area, restrooms, stairs, chimney, storage, closet and gallery.

Essentially a tube-like structure, the primary space seems to form a natural funnel or passage leading into and out of the secondary space. At every turning point the building is visually open through transparent glass walls, affording the entry of natural light and majestic views of the surrounding forest.

The structure is of wood but deviates from the traditional building system. Using ship-shaped elements, each element contains a secondary space inside it which interactively sustains the roof to shelter the unified building.

Because the roof plates are composed of a series of differentiated small beams, it could easily accept any irregular plane, though three-dimensionally distorted. The construction procedure has, therefore, been simplified and made less expensive.

1

Satoshi Okada Architects

1 View from road at front; in summer building is hidden
   under tree canopy
2 Rear view with large openings faces primeval forest
3 View from east
4 Façade at dawn

2

3

4

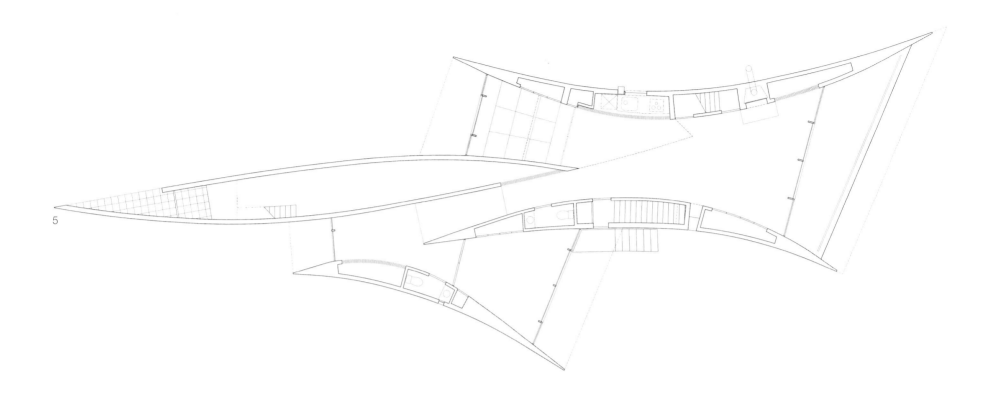

5

6

7

8

9

5 Ground-floor plan; ship-shape elements
   function as structure that contains the
   secondary space
6 View from entry
7 Entrance space is compressed with
   vertical expansion of gallery behind
8 Bathroom and terrace
9 Terrace with views of primeval forest best
   viewed from this level

10 West elevation
11 Living and dining space; dining space is compressed by loft above
12 Entrance gallery; from floor level, wall curves inward at height of 2.2 metres in convex fashion
13 Living space
14 Loft and dining room. Kitchen is behind vertical blinds next to dining area
Photography: Satoshi Okada & Nacasa & Partners

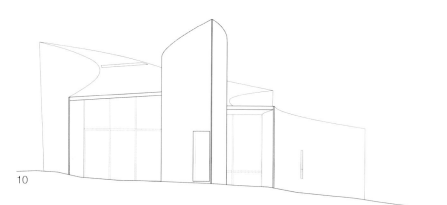

10

11

12

13

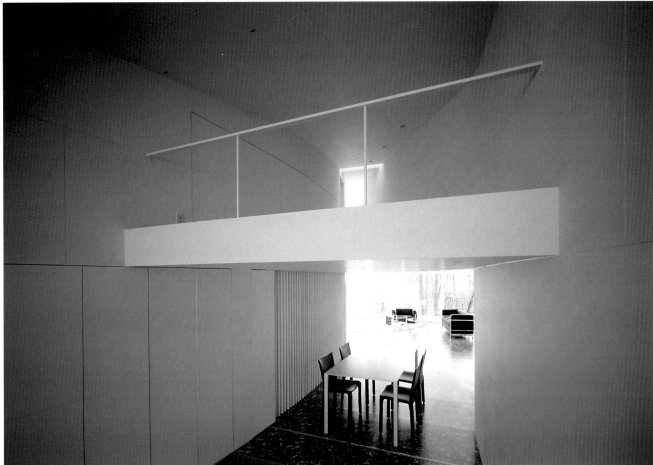

14

Heart of the Home

This compact apartment in Amsterdam has been rebuilt into a luxurious home. The design's key elements and their functions were derived from the distinguishing characteristics of the owner. In the project 'Heart of the Home', the most important feature is that the unit is a compact box, a 'living machine' with a household around it.

The apartment is divided into three zones: front (kitchen, eating, social), middle (living and relaxing) and back (sleeping and reading). The sleeping and living areas are located towards the garden. The front area is adjacent to the public street. In the absence of walls and dividing objects, these different areas are still clearly defined.

The design is minimalist and finely detailed. By coordinating all cupboards in the bathroom and kitchen, the space can be viewed as a whole. All fronts and doors have been made without handles to express the autonomy of the object. The materials and design were chosen to enhance the compact and minimalist nature of the interior.

A unique feature of the apartment is the bathroom at the core, which was nominated for the Netherlands bathroom design award. The overall design called for a clever solution to a complex commission, and the architects' response was a skilful layout within the spatial context.

1

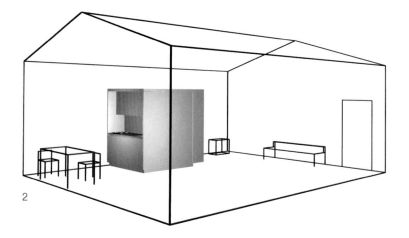

2

1   Living and relaxing zone
2   3D visual 'living machine'
3   Front view apartment
Photography: i29 office for design

i29 office for design

House in Aroeira

Perfectly integrated into its surroundings, this single-family house is located in Aroeira. The site lies within a beautiful preservation area, 21 kilometres from Lisbon and 600 metres from a stretch of sandy beach. Aroeira is famed for its large golf resort: a fully enclosed 345-hectare property set in a mature pine forest. This house nestles into the Aroeira Estate, a few kilometres away from the golf course and beaches of Fonte da Telha. The location makes it a perfect setting for relaxation and leisure, with close proximity to the city centre.

This two-storey structure with additional basement was designed to provide multifunctional use of the social areas. The lower floor comprises a main hall that leads to the kitchen, service area, family room, living room and dining room. The social areas lean over a relaxation area that includes an exterior terrace with a wooden floor deck and swimming pool. The upper floor includes four bedrooms, two bathrooms and a master bedroom suite.

The two main vertical spaces of the house symbolise the 'modern' versus the 'traditional'. Connection between them is through a central cubic glass space clad with horizontal wooden louvres that provide an interesting shade element. The modern area leads to the swimming pool, and includes an upper terrace roof from which the second storey can be accessed. The traditional area has a tiled roof that gives it a country-style image and encompasses the four bedrooms.

One of the main considerations when designing the house was to provide a high-quality standard for exterior spaces to include landscape views. Architecture and construction materials were also taken into account and met the same high standards. These factors collectively maximise privacy and security levels while making the best use of garden and exterior settings.

The carefully planned connection between the interior and exterior of the house permits access to all the exterior lounging areas: terraces, gardens and patio, at different levels. All these areas lead to the swimming pool and are accessible from almost all areas of the house.

1

1 Detail of exterior walls clad in Barroncos shale
2 View of living space and swimming pool
3 South elevation

3

4 View of surrounding area
5 Main stairway leading to bedrooms
6 Detail of skylight in ensuite
Photography: FG + SG | Fotografia de Arquitectura

4

5

6

House in East Hampton

East Hampton, New York, USA

East Hampton is a popular resort area of bays, rivers, marshes and miles of ocean beaches. This house was built for a New York City couple with two young children and a close, extended family. It was designed to accommodate the family during their summer activities in the Hamptons.

The composition of semi-detached structures, reminiscent of the agricultural buildings common on neighbouring farms, provides separation for the multi-generational guests. The structures serve to frame the pool and deck as a social and architectural focus.

Set within a tall pine forest, the house is oriented for full southern exposure. Cedar trellises festooned with wisteria give shade to the first-floor rooms and ample windows direct attention to the pool and patio.

Flanking the pool are an outdoor grille area, a sheltered area for game tables, a built-in spa, and areas for outdoor dining and lounging. With easy access to the pool, a large recreation room is contained in the second floor of the garage. The main section of the house includes the kitchen, living, dining, and media rooms with children's bedrooms on the second floor.

Located in a separate building connected by the main entry, are the master suite and guest room. Upstairs, a private library with fireplace has views to the surrounding woods and over the pool. Space is designed to effortlessly support large groups of people indoors and outdoors.

1 Library
Opposite:
    Southern façade and pool terrace

1

Centerbrook Architects and Planners/William H. Grover, FAIA with Edward J. Keagle, AIA

3 Pool terrace
4 Detail of main house

4

5 Second-floor plan
6 First-floor plan
7 Dining room and kitchen with children's bedroom above
8 Library
9 Dining room with entrance beyond
10 Main entrance
Photography: Jeff Goldberg/Esto Photographics

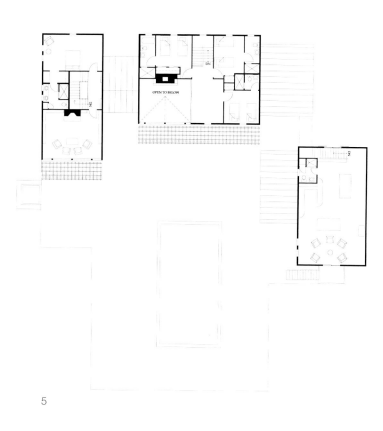

5

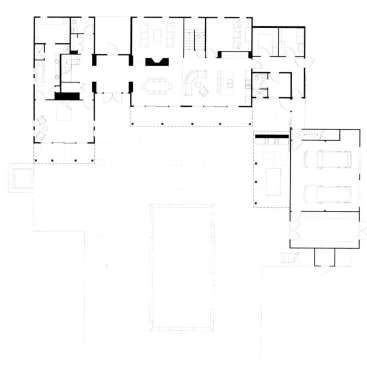

6

7

8

9

10

House in the Hudson Valley

New York, USA

The 19th-century farmhouse that once graced this site has been extensively renovated and extended to form a character-filled weekend retreat. It sits comfortably into the gently rolling hills of upstate New York. The complex now appears as a string of traditional, connected barns from the approaching road. It contains a gymnasium and exercise rooms, a spa, a major room for entertainment, a bunkroom, an office, a summer room, gardens, terraces, and a pool house and pool. The design was intended to transport the owners out of their 'work-a-day' city world to one of maximum physical and emotional comfort.

An informal entry gate leads into an intimate herb garden where views of the whole complex unfold. Stone walls create outdoor terraces and places to sit overlooking the pool and pond. Inside, fir panelling and stylised 'trees' used in the entertainment room recall the owners' love of Adirondack lodges and the forests that surround their property.

The bunkroom perches like a tree house in the upper reaches of the major entertainment room. Triple-hung windows convert the summer room into a screen porch on pleasant days. The gymnasium contains a half-court for basketball and a windowed exercise room overlooking the vegetable garden. A private view of a relaxing, miniature Zen rock garden is featured from the spa's jucuzzi tub. Commanding panoramic views of the property, the office has its own outdoor entrance.

The extensive use of stone and exposed beams maintain a rustic and cosy ambience, delivered with a contemporary flair. The 19th-century character of the original has been echoed in conservatory type features. Furniture, fireplace accessories and lighting were also designed by Centerbrook and enhance the concept and integrity of their overall design.

1   Nineteenth-century farmhouse at left, addition at right
Opposite:
    View from garden

1

Centerbrook Architects and Planners/Jefferson B. Riley, FAIA and Charles G. Mueller, AIA

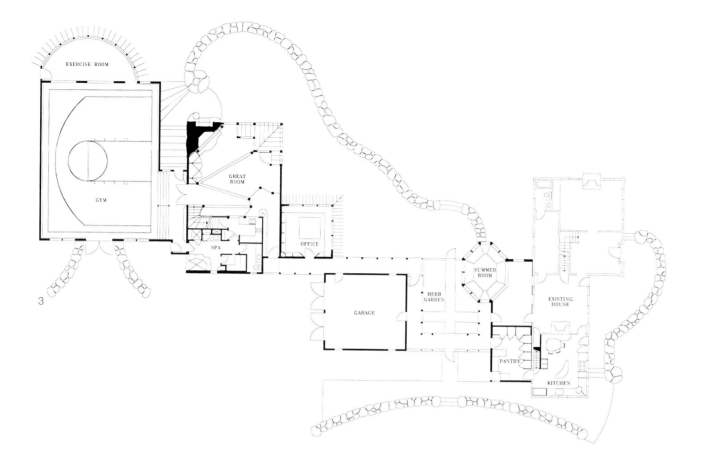

3

4

5

6

6 Entertainment room seen from second floor
7 Bunkroom above entertainment room
8 Entertainment room
9 Summer room
10 Kitchen
Photography: Brian Vanden Brink

7

8

9

10

House in Regua

This house is located in Peso da Régua in the heart of the Douro region in northern Portugal. The region is valued as one of the most ancient in Europe. Backed by the Serra do Marão mountains and overlooking the wide valley of the River Douro, the peaceful town of Peso da Régua is the official centre of the port wine-growing region. In this region, the vines are grown on terraced slopes leading down to the river, providing visitors with a series of spectacular views, which can be admired from the area's many viewpoints.

Due to its distinctive contemporary features the design of the house is considered a landmark in the area. Set on an accentuated northwest to southeast slope, it was designed to high standards with both its interior and exterior spaces, along with site landscaping and building of excellent quality. The design features offer maximum privacy and security and take advantage of the views, exposure to the sun and the surrounding garden.

The site provided one of the restrictions for the house, occupying a polygon-shaped block as defined by the building regulations of the city. As a strategy, the designer gave the house a balanced distribution of the different areas, which helped to compensate for the restriction.

The house is organised on two levels, with an additional basement. Its north elevation is at a lower height with two apparent levels, compared to the three visible levels on the south elevation. On this side, the house is characterised by a series of spaces that, by means of protruding bodies or voids, attempts to give a different character to the slope. This appears to reduce the size of the overall mass, making it seem visually smaller than it really is.

As defined by the client, the project is essentially a four-bedroom home and office. The main entrance is located on the south elevation. Entry is gained via an exterior stairway reaching the first level and leading into the hall. This hall is the focal point of the interior space. It encompasses the main staircase that visually and physically connects all the levels by means of stairs, balconies and voids. The living room is the main focus of the house by both its exterior volume and spatial characteristics. It faces south towards the main exterior views, and has a two-floor height with a large glass pane feature window. The garden is accessed from this level through the living room or kitchen. The garden surrounds the whole house with the larger portion on the north side that includes the swimming pool. A small hall and an L-shaped balcony surrounded by four bedrooms, each with its own bathroom, are located on the upper floor.

The deep interior/exterior connection is well represented in the large, open terrace area, ending where the swimming pool is located. Having access from the living room or bedrooms, the pool is a direct extension of the house.

The house is an elegant and contemporary home with traditional features derived from the materials and colours. The different spaces and floors of the house integrate it perfectly with its surroundings. The large windows merge the ravishing exterior views with the interior of the house. It is the ideal setting to relax and enjoy the view, over a glass of wine from the Douro region.

1

2

1 Exterior view
2 Overhead view of lounge area
3 View of living space and swimming
  pool
Photography: FG + SG | Fotografia de
Arquitectura

3

House on the Maine Coast

Maine, USA

Facing the water with beautiful views of Blue Hill Harbor in Maine, this house emerges from a rocky promontory. The orientation is to the west looking across the harbour to Blue Hill village, a quintessential settlement on the Penobscot Bay seacoast.

From the road, the house is approached from a courtyard between the entry façade and nearby garage. Gathered under a large-hipped roof that exudes a feeling of shelter, the building appears to rise from the rocks. The roof is penetrated by a number of tall, capped chimneys. Windows also emerge from the roof affording the rooms an inspiring vista.

1

1 View from pool and gardens
Opposite:
   View from Penobscot Bay

The large stone terrace on the western side offers a spectacular view of the harbor and from here access can be gained to a landing dock at the water's edge. The north side of the house looks out to gardens and a swimming pool, while the south side is forested with white pines.

The house is clad in stained white cedar shingles and red cedar trim, with a roof of asphalt shingles. Entry from the foyer passes a mudroom before opening into a large central hall. The hall is a major focus for the house and the point of orientation for surrounding rooms. In the hall a curved staircase traces its winding path up past landings to the upper reaches of the house. A large dormer window set high in the ceiling spills sunlight down through this space illuminating the expanse of the decorative chimney and stairs. The chimney has *bas-relief* crisscrossed boards reflective of the hall's floor pattern.

Large interior windows act as scoops capturing secondary light from the central hall and conveying it to the master bedroom and two guest bedrooms. The master bedroom opens to a deck, offering extraordinary views of the harbour. The living room is the only area of the house that breaks out from under the all-encompassing hipped roof. It is a large room with a tray ceiling with French doors that open out to the stone terrace.

Finishes in the hall, living room, kitchen and elsewhere employ beaded board and other materials that resonate with the traditions of Penobscot Bay. The design for this house creates spaces that explore volume and light.

Centerbrook Architects and Planners/Chad Floyd, FAIA

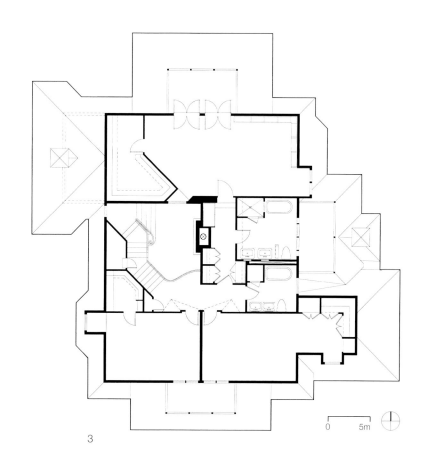

3

0   5m

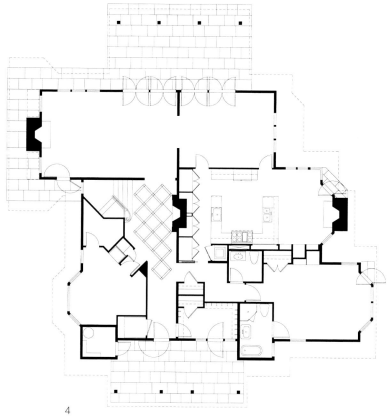

4

5

6

7

8

9

10

9 Central hall
10 Master bedroom
Photography: Jeff Goldberg/Esto Photographics

Island House

Vancouver Island, British Columbia, Canada

This house was designed as a vacation house for an extended family. Perched on a steep bank, it overlooks a protected ocean harbour on Vancouver Island's south coast. Summers spent at the original cabin on site provided the clients with intimate knowledge of the prevalent conditions. Breezes, light and vegetation were all considered in the design of the house. Care was taken to preserve an established orchard, vegetable garden and existing trees. Places in the previous cabin used for favourite activities such as the reading and yoga areas on the morning deck were rebuilt into the new house. Also retained were the outdoor summer cooking area on the western deck, an open fire-pit near the beach stairs for those starlit meals and late night conversations and play areas around a massive rock. This resulted in a new home with a feeling of familiarity.

The main house has an area of 225 square metres with a 75-square-metre office and bedroom wing. Three of the bedrooms are designed with a dual purpose: wall-beds fold down from built-in office casework. The guest bedroom and office wing is connected to the main house with a covered breezeway and provides acoustic separation. The generous living and dining area is flanked by a kitchen, pantry, laundry and bathroom. An oversized Rumford fireplace forms the focal point of the main living area, and contrasts with the small adjacent inglenook.

Thick poured-in-place concrete walls create a casual, robust and quiet house. A feeling of simultaneous weight and airiness is provided to the interior and exterior by the combination of concrete walls and full-height aluminium windows. Steel connections stiffen the timber frame, and separate structural elements form a theme carried throughout with dissimilar materials and textures never touching. Polished concrete floors with radiant heating contrast with the rough concrete walls. Polished exterior slabs extend living areas to the exterior.

Exterior and interior materials were chosen for longevity and all building materials were sourced locally.

Because the climate is very dry in this region with long hot summers, large overhangs are tuned to annual sun angles, preventing overheating in summer. A simple mono-pitch roof rises to the west permitting low winter sun to penetrate deep within the building. Thick concrete walls act as thermal mass in cool and hot seasons, storing heat and cold to be released throughout the building when temperatures change. Cross-ventilation from carefully placed windows catch onshore and offshore breezes, aiding summer cooling. Rainwater from a gutter that runs the entire width of the house is directed down chain leaders to irrigate indigenous plants and trees.

The porous edges that abut surrounding vegetation provide the house with a calm and quiet presence. Though still relatively new, the house is at ease in its setting. Its roughness has the appeal of a well used and appreciated home.

1

D'Arcy Jones Design Inc

3 View from kitchen area towards dining and living areas
4 Master bedroom viewed from exterior
5 Dining area viewed from outdoor terrace
6 View from outdoor terrace towards master bedroom

3

4

5

6

7

8

7 Main entry viewed from outdoor terrace
8 Floating cedar bench with fire pit beyond
9 Outdoor terrace viewed from master bedroom
Photography: D'Arcy Jones (1, 5, 7, 8 & 9),
    Martin Tessler (2, 3, 4 & 6)

9

Kent Residence

Rancho Mirage, California, USA

The Kent Residence is in a residential, gated community estate occupying a site of approximately 0.5 hectares. The design brief for this residence was to create a spacious, luxurious desert residential estate with guest house, pavilion, tennis court, pool and spa of an untraditional, unique and sophisticated character.

The main residence has a guest bedroom, maid's room, large living room, office, dining room, kitchen with butler's pantry, breakfast room and a master suite with his and her separate bathrooms. It also hosts an exercise room. The guesthouse is connected to a tennis pavilion and has two bedrooms with attached bathrooms.

This lavish contemporary estate was designed for entertainment. The front of the house has a ceremonial raised entry with large planters covered in coral stone-finished texture. Entry is gained to the house via a bridge over a reflecting pool. A sculptural entry gate welcomes visitors. Portion of the semi-circular gate is partly suspended over a reflecting pool, stretching towards the dining room.

The design of the residence affords the visitor a new and revealing experience with every step. The entry foyer has a vaulted ceiling with architectural cove lighting. Southern overhangs keep the hot desert sun out during the summer months and allow sunshine to enter in winter. To take advantage of the solar orientation, overhangs also let sunshine enter on the front reflecting pool effectively reflecting it back up onto the multi-levelled ceiling. Coral stone-finished columns further accentuate the entry foyer.

The ceiling of the large living room is clear cedar, providing exceptional acoustics for an entertainment centre with an audio/video system. A spectacular sculptural ceiling features in the banquet-size dining room. The kitchen and breakfast room have generous glass areas to receive the morning sun and capture the mountain view.

The placement of the media room with sunken bar also takes advantage of the mountain views. The master suite has a private workout room and includes a sunken sitting room and cosy fireplace.

Exterior stone decking leads to the guesthouse and pavilion designed for outdoor entertainment and fitted with all kitchen amenities. The pavilion is located between the pool area and the sunken tennis court. There is a feeling of a magical retreat created within this area, featuring a multi-levelled pool and spa fed by cascading waterfalls. Raised marble-covered planters and spacious patio areas give a choice for quality, pampering privacy or selective socialising.

Even though the house has been designed for luxury, equal attention has been paid to making it energy-efficient. The building has a heavy emphasis on large amounts of glass both inside and out allowing the transfer of light and unobstructed views. It is an untraditional desert home with a strong, contemporary Mediterranean character: both monumental and strongly geometric.

1

Patel Architecture/Narendra Patel AIA

1 Multi-levelled pool and spa combine with waterfalls, raised planters and spacious patios – all designed to create the sounds and feel of a magical retreat
2 Spacious great room with wood ceiling includes entertainment centre, two-sided fireplace and plenty of lounge space

Kumu Honua

Honolulu, Hawaii, USA

This corporate guest residence is located on one of Hawaii's most spectacular beachfronts. The location commands sweeping views of the ocean and landforms beyond, making the setting a driving force behind the design concept. This 1150-square-metre home was designed to complement and frame the dramatic natural landscape.

A continually widening progression of experiences is revealed when moving from the raised entry pavilion through corridors that frame a central courtyard towards living areas fronting the ocean.

The water features that originate at the entry and connect to pools around the courtyard 'float' the edges of the building, providing a sense of tranquillity and connection to the ocean beyond. Full-height glass walls under wide roof overhangs provide subtle natural light throughout the interior spaces and add to the sense of indoor/outdoor living.

The interior is one of understated elegance. It does not overwhelm or compete with the natural beauty surrounding the residence. Furniture and fabrics were selected for their simplicity and harmony, and provide a warm and neutral background that accentuates the natural surroundings. Bathrooms with private gardens are rich and sumptuous with elegant fixtures and detailing.

A lush tropical landscape surrounds the residence, adding to the feel of luxury, privacy and connection to nature. Granite pavers form a lanai from which the laser-edged swimming pool provides a seemingly seamless connection to the ocean beyond.

1

Previous pages:
Looking northwest across pool from north of lounge wing
4 Entry foyer
5 Lounge area

4

5

6 Corridor in residential wing; entry to courtyard at left
7 Corridor to lounge area in west wing
Photography: Tim Griffith

Landmark Villa

Situated on a high plateau overlooking the Teton Mountain Range, Landmark Villa Townhomes brought unique design challenges to the firm of Dubbe-Moulder Architects. The design project called for the residences, of approximately 487 square metres, to include a two-car garage, master suites, loft area, and three guest suites, each with its own full bathroom. While fitting all of this living space into the small parameters of the lots was a major challenge, it was also paramount for the design to provide access to unparalleled views of the Teton mountain range.

The resulting designs put the garage and public areas of each townhouse on the ground level. The master bedroom and guest suites were put on different levels in each townhouse to best work with each site's views and proximity to neighbouring properties. Massive windows on the main floor open the living area to spectacular Teton views, while a covered deck opening from the living area allows for entertaining during the warm summer months.

The exteriors of each townhouse emulate the European alpine style of architecture as well as the great mountain lodges of the Pacific northwestern national parks. They combine Douglas fir logs, horizontal Douglas fir plank and chink siding, and western red cedar shingle siding. Massive fireplaces constructed of Oklahoma farmer block stone have mantels supported by logs with the mantel itself a round log flattened on the upper side. The two townhouses have a distinct, architectural texture that integrates well with the beautiful surroundings of Jackson Hole. Craftsman style elements, such as the diamond cut red cedar shingles, further enhance the exteriors, giving the project the visual impact of a high-end, custom home.

1

1 Covered porch
2 Living room

Dubbe-Moulder Architects, PC

3

3   Dining room with living room on right
4   View of Teton Range
5   Master bedroom
6   Kitchen
Photography: Ed Prater (1,4),
    Dubbe-Moulder Archtects, PC (2,3,5,6)

4

5

6

Landrin Residence

'Les Collines', Petion-Ville, Haiti

The site for this residence is one of the highest points of the 'Les Collines' residential development project. The hilly location offers panoramic views all around and an ideal location to capture winds blowing in from the plains.

The main views are of the plains towards the border of the Dominican Republic to the east, the mountains of Petion-Ville to the south/southwest, and the Port-au-Prince bay area at the west/southwest. The front/main façade and terrace of the house faces east and the back of the house faces west.

The site is very steep. Height differs by about eight metres from the lowest point at the street entrance level and the highest point at the rear.

Construction in Haiti is limited to locally available materials. Pre-fabricated items are not easily available. The house is a post and beam structure with all interior and exterior walls made of 15-centimetre cinder blocks with mortar stucco/plastering on both sides. Columns and beams are poured in place using reinforced concrete. The entire structure looks strong and resilient.

The site conditions of a warm and windy climate and inspiring views were taken into consideration at the design stage. All rooms benefit from the view; the front to the surrounding plains and back to the mountains and bay. Additionally, the living/dining room has large windows opening to front and rear views, with access to both the main front terrace and a back patio. Four rooms, the living, family, additional guest room and bathroom, form part of the first floor plan. This level also includes the kitchen, dining, laundry and storage area. On this level, the service staff quarters which adjoin the kitchen are above the garage. They open directly to the outside, providing independent access.

A two-car garage at the lower level ensured the driveway slope would not be too steep. The main front entrance above the garage and driveway allows transition to the first floor and opens to the main entrance and living room area.

Three bedrooms and a family television room are on the second floor along with a master bedroom suite. The master bedroom opens to a small balcony at the front and a private terrace at the back with views to the bay and mountains. The feature windows take in the plains beyond. Two of the other bedrooms on this level offer different views accessing the panorama on the south side.

As the house is not air conditioned, special attention has been given to natural air circulation. Each room opens on two or more sides for maximum cross ventilation.

At both the front and back of the house landscaping and stone retaining walls create flat areas. The front level area is a garden with contained lawn, directly accessible from the driveway or the main front terrace. The back level area is accessed via a door in the dining room and through walkways around the house paved with red-brick-tiles. The rest of the site is treated as a natural 'sloped' garden.

1 Rear façade. Second floor master bedroom balcony is over first floor kitchen
2 Front façade; view from street level with driveway. Stone retaining wall creates front garden area
3 Front terrace with view to east towards the plains and the Dominican Republic

1

2

3

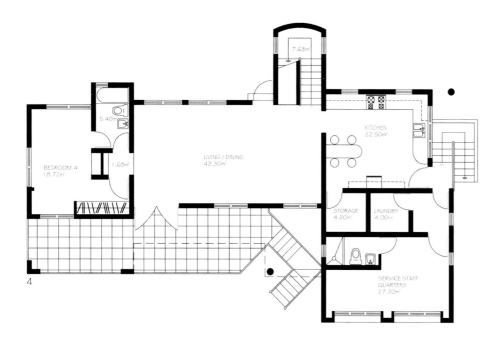

BEDROOM 4
18.72m²

5.40m²

1.68m²

LIVING / DINING
42.30m²

7.63m²

KITCHEN
22.50m²

STORAGE
4.20m²

LAUNDRY
4.00m²

SERVICE STAFF
QUARTERS
27.20m²

4

BEDROOM 2
19.80m²

6.60m²

FAMILY
39.63m²

WALKING
CLOSET
9.00m²

BALCONY
6.20m²

BEDROOM 3
18.00m²

7.50m²

MASTER BEDROOM
27.93m²

BALCONY
7.20m²

5

7

6

8

4 Second-floor plan
5 First-floor plan
6 Back patio
7 Main entrance door; view from living room to front terrace and scenic panorama beyond
8 Back patio; naturally sloped garden is continued beyond stone retaining wall
9 Living and dining room with view of kitchen beyond; at left, door opens to back patio
Photography: Raphael Izmery, architect

Lieutenant Island Residence

Wellfleet, (Cape Cod), Massachusetts, USA

The primary design objectives for this house were the desire to take advantage of exceptional views, provide a variety of spatial experiences within the confines of a small project, and to embrace the outdoors in the concept of the design. The site for the project was a heavily wooded bluff overlooking Cape Cod Bay. Here pine, bayberry and oak predominate. The house was intended to harmonise with the natural landscape and sit on a base that incorporated timbers, bluestone pavers, and natural grade terraces: to provide a sense that the built environment grew out of the hillside.

The entry side is a platform-framed box. Small punched windows present a private formal façade and enclose the entry hall, stair, kitchen and master bedroom suite. Expanding into a two-storey living-dining room with a large window wall that faces north, the upper area takes in the primary view of Cape Cod Bay. Since the natural gradient of the land rises towards the water, the living room is elevated above the first floor for better access to the view. It also provides a partial enclosure for the dining area with built-in bookcases and seating.

The master bedroom and library on the second floor have balconies that overlook the living room. A deck above the screened porch can be accessed from the bedroom and offers additional views of Cape Cod Bay. A pergola structure affords a shaded outdoor retreat as an alternative to the open terrace.

Two guest bedrooms located off the main public living space have small decks and access to an outdoor shower. Located at the end of the corridor that runs alongside the living room, the office workspace offers privacy and different views of the bay than those seen from the living room due to differing orientation.

Occupied mainly during the summer months, natural ventilation was a critical design concern for this house. The sloping ceiling of the main living space directs warm air to several sets of motorised awning windows which can be opened to let hot air escape. These windows are in turn shielded from rain and sun by the overhanging roof.

1 Exterior view looking towards entry
2 Exterior view looking northeast

1

Hammer Architects

3   First-floor plan
4   Interior view of kitchen, dining area and loft bedroom
5   Interior looking north towards Cape Cod Bay
Photography: Lance Keimig (1, 3, 4 & 5), Mark D. Hammer (2)

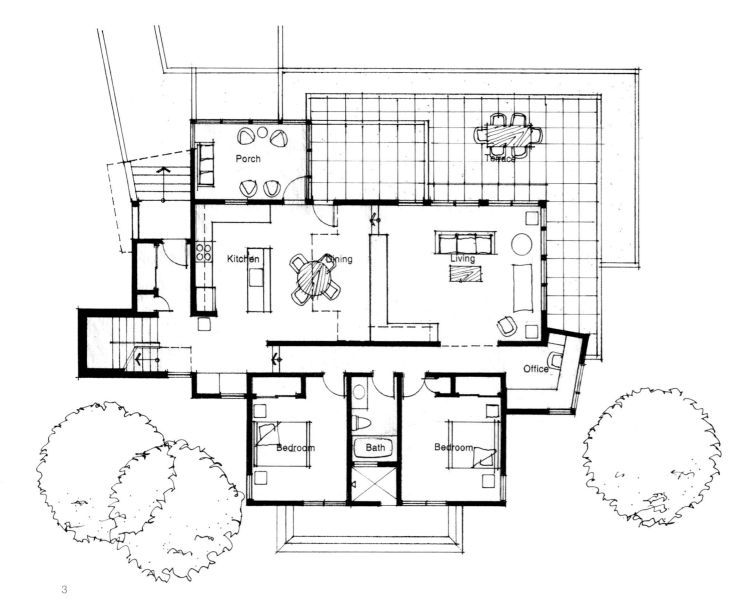

Porch

Terrace

Kitchen

Dining

Living

Office

Bedroom

Bath

Bedroom

3

4

3 Floor plan
4 View through living space to sea
5 Central courtyard deck
6 View to bay

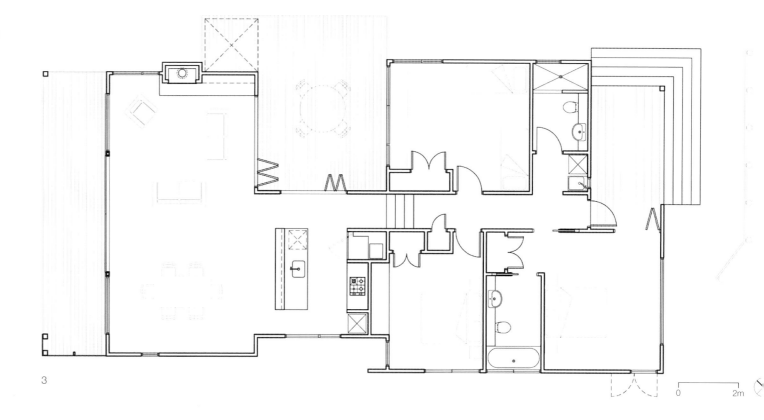

3

0   2m

4

5

7   Ensuite
8   Living space and courtyard
Photography: Paul McCredie

7

8

Longboat Key Beach House

Longboat Key, Florida, USA

This single-family house is located in the Gulf of Mexico on a barrier island near Sarasota, Florida.

Coastal conservation restrictions shaped the location and parameters of the design, necessitating a vertical sloping setback line. The project called for a modest home of approximately 370 square metres.

On the busy road fronting the site, the design created a solid 'wall' of rectangular shapes contrasting with the curves of palms. Large glazed walls open to the Gulf under a solid, covered concrete frame.

The pool, located on the south side of the structure, gains full sun exposure and is designed into the 'base' of the house. Part of the pool is located under the elevated Gulf terrace, creating a reflective space from above. The building is open to light and expansive views, but protected from the strong winds that frequent this area.

1

1 View of living room and master bedroom loft
  looking towards Gulf of Mexico
2 View of house from Gulf of Mexico looking west
3 Master bedroom looking out over living room and
  to suspended exterior private terrace

3

2

4   View of pool on south side looking west. Wall at end affords privacy from street
Opposite:
   Arrival view looking west

4

6 View from dining room looking towards kitchen. Sliding wall on right closes kitchen for entertaining

7 View from kitchen towards dining and living rooms

8 View of two-storey living room looking under concrete frame towards Gulf of Mexico

Photography: Steven Brooke Studios

6

7

1 Pool serves as centrepiece with direct access from all rooms
Opposite:
    Multi-level pool deck area also has swim-up bar, raised planters and entry walkway

Magical Retreat

La Quinta, California, USA

This retreat, located in picturesque surroundings, was designed for a young family with children. The site had a lake view towards the back and mountain views towards the front. The client's desire was a sophisticated, untraditional desert home with a contemporary Mediterranean feel. The design of the house successfully translated the clients' vision into architectural reality and took advantage of both front and back views.

The front gate area of the house creates a ceremonial and welcoming environment for entering guests. Made of sculpturally etched glass, it is then crowned with a welded steel structure supported with poured in place concrete columns.

A spectacular entry courtyard emerges as soon as the front gates are opened, establishing the mood and tone of the house. The pool, which becomes a focal point, creates a dramatic visual experience with every step leading to the entry door. The meandering edge of the reflecting pool and engraved pattern on the walkway surface is characterised by undulating, sweeping curves.

Symbolising permanence, a massive natural rock placed on a slab is used as an entry credenza. Selected for their endurance and low-maintenance properties, materials such as natural stone, steel, wood, glass and water feature predominantly.

The dining room has curved glazing positioned against the reflecting pond and provides a superb view to the lake. A 225-kilogramme glass chandelier is suspended over the glass dining table. The sunken living room has a stone-covered fireplace with a water wall above and was designed to create an intriguing exclamation point with the juxtaposition of fire and water.

The high-performance kitchen has a large glass window with a panoramic lake view that not only provides a breathtaking view while cooking, but also brings in natural light. Elsewhere, soft, subdued lighting creates an atmosphere of warm and inviting cosiness. Additional fixtures like the pool table were custom designed using exotic woods. The pool table has a stainless steel base, illuminated with a suspended inverted cone-shaped cobalt blue light fixture.

The outdoor living space has much visual appeal. A large fireplace, roof overhang with cedar ceiling, a multi-level pool and spa combined with waterfalls and raised planters create the sounds and feel of a magical retreat.

1

Patel Architecture/Narendra Patel, AIA

3   Large, natural rock used as entry credenza. Dining room beyond has blown-glass chandelier
4   Family room and breakfast room are open to kitchen and outdoor area

4

5 Courtyard pool also serves as reflecting pool for entry
6 Pool table is of exotic woods and stainless steel base,
  lighted with suspended inverted cone-shaped light fixtures

5

6

7 Large glass windows in kitchen offer panoramic lake views and bring in natural light
8 Sunken bar overlooks lake

7

10

9 Sunken living room with stone-covered fireplace and water wall above
10 Master bath
11 Master bedroom
Photography: Nicola Pira

11

Modernised Mountain Retreat

Teton County, Wyoming, USA

This rustic home of about 28 squares was built in the 1970s. Recently modernised it has retained all its rustic charm, adding contemporary elegance, convenience and efficiency during its renovation. The changes have expanded the feeling of light and air entering the living space thus giving it the lift and lightness of anticipation as one room opens onto another.

The use of timber, stone and glass is an engaging feature. Approaching the entrance, the glassed-in portico draws visitors in under the inverted prow-like roof which mimics similar roofs on two other sides of the building. The handy 84 square garage has been reorientated with its entrance now pointing away from the front of the building, thus emphasising the charming openness of the design.

1

Renovated around an open plan philosophy, the main generous living space of the house places the kitchen at the northern end. It flows naturally onto a dining area which spills into a cosy open-fired lounge with pleasant nooks for reading, listening to music or whiling away the hours. The tall windows surrounding this area not only express light into the interior of the building, but frame the unobstructed views of mountains to the north and stands of aspen, conifer and cottonwood trees in the surrounding environment. Chunky timber posts and beams give this house a feeling of strength and stability.

The reconfigured bedrooms have access to a pleasing, elegant and roomy bathroom, whilst the new master bedroom opens on to its own private balcony. New woodwork and trim, custom made cabinetry, quality finishes and high-end appliances give this interior a timeless appeal.

Outside dry-stacked Montana moss rock features around the exterior of the home. The stone terrace hosts a barbeque grill surrounded by planters and an extensive outdoor entertainment area.

1 Large windows provide much needed light
2 View of rear exterior

Dubbe-Moulder Architects, PC

3   Light-filled dining room
Opposite:
   Kitchen looking towards dining room

3

178

3   Light-filled dining room
Opposite:
   Kitchen looking towards dining room

3

5   Living room
6   Master bathroom
7   Foyer
Photography: Woolly Bugger Studios

6

7

Private Paradise

The design of this beautiful villa located close to Genoa and a half-hour drive from Portofino was inspired by the magnificent mountain landscape of Liguria. Liguria is a 'ritzy' resort area that is a veritable playground for the rich and famous. A lovely coastline and terraced hillsides covered with olive trees, forests abounding with lemon trees, flowers and herbs and groves of pine and almond trees add to the lure of this charming region.

The owners are well-known Italian actors who sought a haven that offered privacy and a means to escape their frenetic lives in the city. Therefore their home was to be a refuge where they could relax with family and friends in total privacy enjoying the extraordinary landscape of the villa's surroundings.

The house was designed to merge with the landscape. Local stone for the façades and chestnut wood for some structural areas and the interiors ensured that this concept was embraced. Yet, inasmuch as the house appears to be a beautiful mountain villa from the exterior, it holds an intriguing secret. Tucked away in the basement is an area of luxurious relaxation with a swimming pool, hydro massage, aero massages and sauna. This space is completely hidden from the rest of the house.

Elsewhere the house projects an air of total tranquillity with its interiors reflecting understated elegance.

1

Roberto Silvestri Architetto with Maria Previti

1 View from southeast; two different volumes inside each
   other recall the old, local farm architectural vernacular
2 Stone façade built using stone from mountains in
   background

3 Plans
4 Contemporary and traditional design merge together in living room
5 Dining room with glazing on two sides
6 Kitchen built on site using bricks for cooking area and Cardoso stone for flooring
7 Private paradise: located underground, a relaxation zone with swimming pool, spa, sauna, hydro massage and aero massage
8 Guest bedroom on upper floor
Photography: Roberto Silvestri

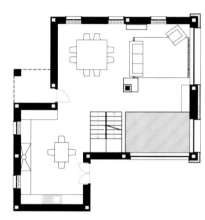

5

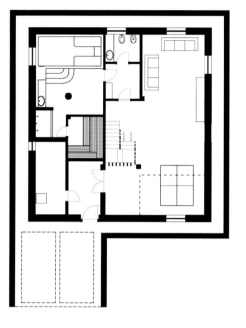

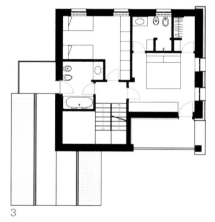

3

4

6

7

8

Residence at Waterford

Rancho Mirage, California, USA

The intention behind the design of this house is an emphasis on its location near water. The materials used, together with a plan that features terraces and patios, lines of sight, sunrises and sunsets, encourages a constant awareness of its setting near water.

This residence, Rancho Mirage, was designed for a Chicago client. It is sited in aptly named Waterford, California. The main living spaces are contained under a sweeping, curved room covered with copper, which will eventually age with patina. The entire roof is lifted creating an illusion of space, and having the effect of bringing the outdoors in. All rooms in the house open out to the patios and pool terraces. Designed for outdoor living, these terraces provide pleasant places to read, dine, and to enjoy sun, cocktails and conversation.

Sites by the lake provide magical vantage points from which to enjoy views of the water and mountains. The layout of this house is organised as a cluster of interconnected parts with overlapping fragments, evoking images of a seaside village with courtyards and terraces. The house is orientated specifically to maximise views and ensure that the sun hits the house at an angle at which its rays are least intense. An atrium forms the heart of the house bringing in natural light, illuminating the interior, and providing cross-ventilation.

The house skilfully frames views of the water and the mountains. Windows reflect water activity indoors in the form of a transparent glimmer or dramatic, dancing refraction. Reflections from the calm surface of this natural body of water and the interplay of light and movement, induces a sense of tranquil wonder. Floating in the pool beside the lake, surrounded by spectacular views, creates a unique, relaxing experience.

1

Patel Architecture/Narendra Patel FAIA

3   Infinity-edge pool designed to give illusion that it is part of lake
4   All rooms in house open out to patios and pool terraces and afford lake views
Following pages:
    House has as many outdoor areas as indoor spaces

3

6 Outdoors and indoors blend seamlessly together
7 Kitchen filled with natural light from insulated skylight
Following pages:
    Main living/great room opens on both sides and is contained under sweeping, curved roof
Photography: Nicola Pira

6

Residence in Iporanga

Guarujá, São Paulo, Brazil

This house is positioned on the site to take advantage of spectacular views. The site is fragile, so the architect decided upon a structure with few points of contact with the ground.

At ground level the housekeeper's quarters, outside play space for the children and garages sit into the landscape. This level also features the geometric swimming pool and outdoor covered play area.

On the first floor, the living room shares its space with a gourmet kitchen. On the other side four bedrooms and the bathrooms are conveniently located. The master bedroom is placed out over a balcony area taking full advantage of the view.

This is a clean structure made with natural materials. The availability of light, air and superb views has been skilfully integrated into this design.

1   Entry access
Opposite:
    Garden and swimming pool with beach beyond

Gui Mattos Arquitetura with Eduardo Kenji, Gustavo Bergmann and Camilla Saba

3 Elevation
4 Overall view of house
5 Third-floor master bedroom balcony
   overlooks ocean

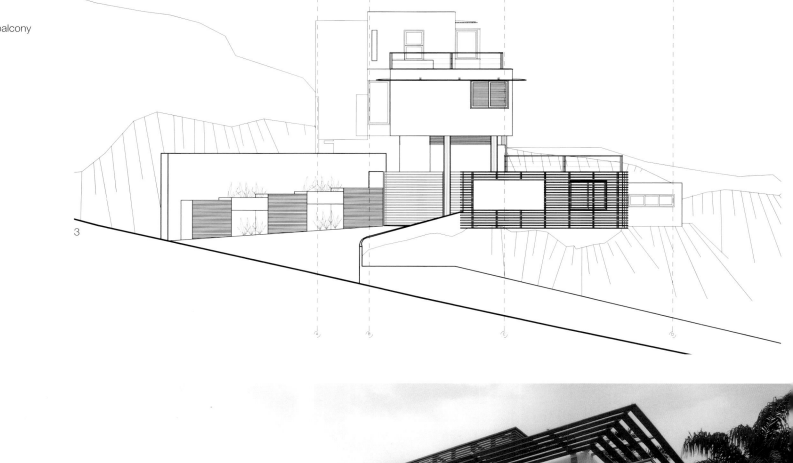

3

4

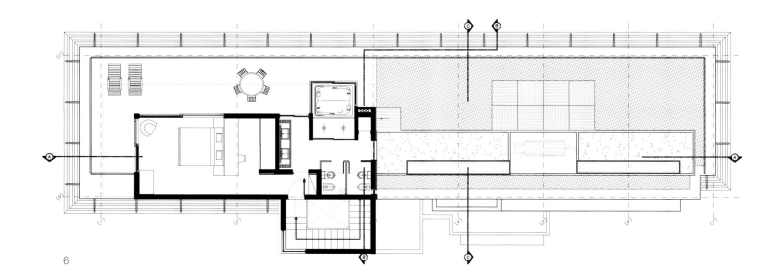

6

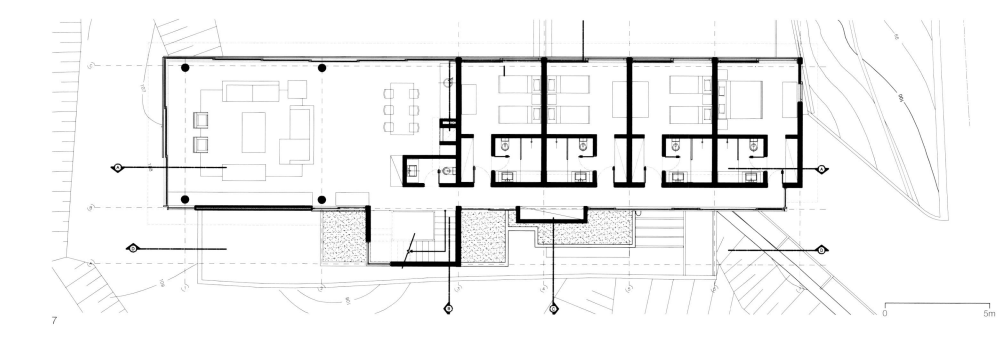

7

0   5m

6 First-floor plan
7 Ground-floor plan
8 Wood details in living area
9 Open spaces blend with outdoors. Natural fibre roof and wood furniture contrast with other material such as acrylic on benches and chairs
10 Living room
Photography: Tuca Reinés

8

9

10

Reviving a Relic

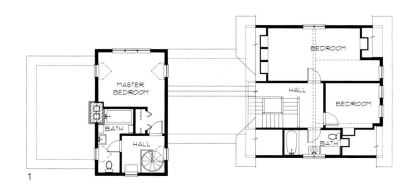

1   Second-floor plan
2   First-floor plan
3   Covered entryway
4   Sunroom
5   Rear exterior
Photography: Dubbe-Moulder Architects, PC

On the west slope of the Teton Mountains in Idaho, in a mature forest of aspen and fir, a small family retreat grows out of the remains of a late 19th-century hand-hewn log homestead that was moved to the site. Modest new connecting elements of wood and native stone in the reclaimed barn tie the cabins together into a gathering place resonating with generations of occupation.

With the one-and-a-half storey reclaimed cabin at the centre of the home, adding a wing for the kitchen, a garage with two bedrooms and a bathroom above expanded the living space. The view overlooks the valley. Seven new courses of logs were added to the half storey to form a full second-storey master bedroom suite. The new spruce logs were machine-flattened on two sides, given a rough, rustic look and an antique finish was applied to blend the new logs seamlessly with the existing logs. The goal of the design was not to create a reproduction, but to incorporate this historic relic to include many of today's modern amenities: hydronic heated floors and an Aga cast-iron radiant heat range.

Woven into, and growing out of its mountain setting, the traditional exterior is well complemented by an eclectic and contemporary interior. Juxtaposing textures and time periods create a unique style, coined as modern rustic. Mixed and matched furnishings, light fixtures and other rustic details add to the character of this residence.

Dubbe-Moulder Architects, PC

3

4

5

Rue de Prince Residence

Edwards, Colorado, USA

This home, inspired by French country estate design sits on top of the Cordillera Rocky Mountains in central Colorado. The site is in a development that has its roots in the regions of central and southern Europe. The style of the development is best illustrated by the traditional design of rural buildings found in Belgium, the Catalonian region of Spain and the southern and central provinces of France. The site was located in an area of magnificent natural beauty and offered breathtaking views of the Cordillera Rocky Mountains.

The design objective of the home was a simple structure with repetitive forms in the French country style. Open floor plans, symmetrically balanced, had to capture the spectacular vistas of the surrounding valleys and mountain ranges from every room.

The house is essentially a 390-square-metre, one-bedroom structure that can accommodate guests in quarters located above the garage.

Entering the home, one steps down into the great room featuring a stone fireplace, expansive windows and detailed trusses capped with wrought iron. The ceiling peaks to a height of 5.5 metres. An open floor plan flows easily to the dining room and kitchen.

Architectural details such as the dining room's coffered ceiling and wrought iron rails provide separation of spaces. The kitchen's island is 'sandy beach' slab granite with a ceramic backsplash. A hearth room is located off the kitchen. The master bedroom suite and a study are also located on the main level. Two additional bedroom suites with an adjacent sitting room are located upstairs.

1

Paddle Creek Design/Thomas H. Oppelt

3 Ground-floor plan
4 Great room fireplace
5 Outdoor living area at kitchen

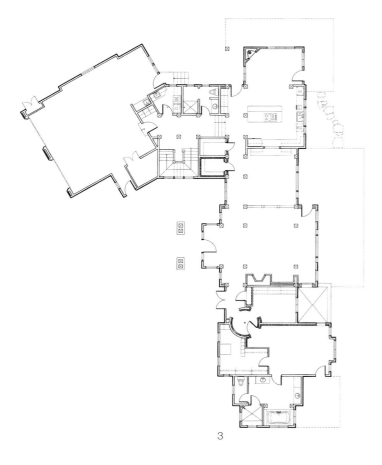

3

4

6　Great room with dining area beyond
7　Dining area with passage through to kitchen

6

8

8 Kitchen – Cordillera valley view beyond
9 Master bedroom
Photography: David O. Marlow

Sanderling Beach House

Siesta Key, Florida, USA

This project called for a multi-level, single-family residence for a family of four to be constructed on the gulf-front of a barrier island on Florida's west coast. The main living spaces are located on the first living level above the flood elevation required for coastal construction. This level includes a children's wing, and quarters for a live-in assistant. Major gulf-front views are provided to all living spaces with controlled internal site views for the children's area. The master bedroom suite, gym, library and guest quarters are located on the upper level, also with views to the gulf-front but additionally to the east side. The rooftop-landscaped terrace overlooks private gardens and a lagoon.

Upon entry down a long formal driveway, the house is designed to unfold from behind the trees. A low wall on the same axis anchors the sky and horizon. The interior space, contained within coloured concrete 'cubes', floats within columns. Between the cubes and concrete frame, a glass curtain wall system completes the enclosure.

The interior functions of the house are defined by the 3-dimensional coloured cubes. Purple represents the public spaces such as the formal living room for entertaining. The guest suite on the upper level is also defined as purple. The orange cube represents the children's area containing their bedrooms and separate bathrooms. The roof of the orange cube serves as a private roof garden that has access from the master bedroom and library. The ochre cube contains family spaces such as kitchen, laundry and family room. The upper level houses the master suite. The white cube is also the central element of the house and as such is the only symmetrical element. The white wall on the ground level serves to anchor the house to the ground and provide a separation between the arrival side of the house and the private beach side.

1

Guy Peterson/Office for Architecture–Guy W. Peterson, FAIA

2

3

4

5

3 Detailed view from west
4 Second level access to purple cube
5 Second level access to roof garden
6 Foyer open to all three levels
7 Living area
Photography: Steven Brooke Studios

6

7

Serenity on the Highway
Tel Aviv, Israel

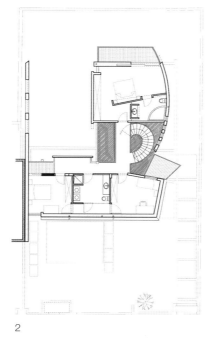

The Kakal Street House is located on a main road in a suburb of Tel Aviv. It is not an ideal location for the occupant who seeks privacy and quiet.

A 'shell' was created to offer both protection and seclusion, addressing the challenge of the adverse circumstances facing this building site. The house and garden combine to form a single unit between the sloped, sealed walls.

An inner courtyard offers a place of seclusion, peace and serenity despite the tumultuous environment that lies beyond its walls. Curved walls and the sweep of the curved staircase detract from the bunker-like feel of the outer shell of the building. Although glass is not heavily emphasised, it is strategically placed to capture light and afford glimpses of the sky beyond.

The architect successfully realised the objective of this building; merging public and private spaces, and offering a haven for family relaxation.

1 Ground-floor plan
2 First-floor plan
3 Façade towards noisy street
4 Garden at daytime
5 Entry
6 Sealed façade towards street
7 Garden at night
8 View from entrance with stairway and inner bridge
9 Ground-floor view towards garden
Photography: Amit Geron

Arcod Architects

4

5

6

7

8

9

Simplicity

Simplicity is nestled in a grove of white cedar trees, interspersed among rocks and facing the ocean. Pasture Bay beach is a mere 60 metres away while Simplicity beach is 182 metres. Both can be reached by a path that meanders through the natural landscape.

The house consists of three large bedrooms, roughly equivalent in size, but each separate and individual in character. Each bedroom has its own private, outdoor space. The large living room (equipped with books, games, stereo, television and video) is open to the sea on one side; the extensive porch and cedar grove on the other. The dining room leads to a courtyard with rock fountain, a swimming pool, sunbathing terrace and pergola. A well-equipped kitchen opens onto its own courtyard complete with herb garden. The house contains a staff cottage for a cook, maid and gardener, as well as a double carport.

The grounds have been carefully landscaped to preserve the natural vegetation as much as possible. Oleander, bougainvillaea, frangipani, thunbergia and other tropical shrubs and trees enhance this natural landscape. Tropical fruit trees such as lime, orange, grapefruit, papaya, banana, avocado and mango thrive on terraces along with a small pineapple plantation and asparagus bed.

The sea breeze is used to its fullest advantage in this construction design. The design provides cool interiors and affords spacious tropical comfort, informality and extraordinary views of the land and seascape.

1

1   View to north up to living room above third bedroom
2   View to southwest across pool towards living room
Following pages
    View southeast towards living room

A.J. Diamond, Donald Schmitt & Company

4

5

6

7 Large windows throughout provide
   ample ventilation
8 Living room viewed from terrace
   above third bedroom
9 Living room
Photography: Tim Griffith

7

8

9

Storm Mountain Fishing Lodge

Steamboat Springs, Colorado, USA

Storm Mountain Fishing Lodge is located in a national park and is designed in the 'Park-itechture Tradition'. This 1000-metre residence draws its historical precedence from two of the great lodges of the west: The Old Faithful Lodge in Yellowstone National Park in Montana and the luxurious Ahwanee Lodge in Yosemite National Park, California. This lodge embraces the vision of Storm Mountain Ranch by incorporating native landscaping and local colours and materials to make the home feel a part of its environment. The objective was to create a home that gives the appearance of being timeless and also to have evolved over a significant period: a home that springs from the landscape rather than have been dropped onto it.

To achieve this sense of being one with nature, the Storm Mountain Fishing Lodge is integrated into the hillside. Locally quarried granite boulders help to create the landscape around the home and stone is used to assist the feeling of transition from nature to the structure. A ballet of man and nature, accomplished by incorporating a variety of native trees, streams and ponds that further the sensual relationship with nature was thus created.

The house is composed of two units connected by a bridge over the roadway. The ground floor contains the great room, kitchen, dining, breakfast, pantry, home-office and garage. Over the bridge, a guest suite used by the owner ensures privacy. This suite is detailed to look like a historic trapper's cabin.

The lower floor contains a bunkroom and a bedroom, a family/media room, children's play room and arcade and a powder room fashioned after an old, outdoor bath. It also contains a guest bedroom, laundry, exercise room and locker room that makes changing clothes and walking out to

the hot tub or man-made beach simple. The large circular stairway connects the exercise room to the master suite. The upper floor contains the master suite, laundry/craft room and 'the roost', a private lounge and two bedrooms.

Rustic materials such as dry-stacked stone for a sense of permanence, round logs for a reflection of pioneer days and a dove tailed square log siding for a more refined, luxurious and contemporary feel completes a large part of the structure. Touches of board and batten, vertical siding and horizontal wavy board siding gives the home another layer of time and evolution visible even in the roof materials. The major part of the roof is tile accented with areas of metal that simulate addition to the original structure over time.

The architectural success of this home is not measured simply by its visual impact but also by the ambience it conveys. 'Tranquil restoration' is evident in the rustic warmth and serenity that comes from a seamless union of architecture and nature.

1

Paddle Creek Design/Thomas H. Oppelt

3

4

5

6

7

8

9

11

12

13   Master bath
14   Sanctuary guest suite
Photography: Sam Belling

13

14

Teton Treasure

The design scheme for this residence was based on a modern adaptation of the typical, western ranch home. The architect created three distinct zones in the house: the private and public areas and guest wing. The private area includes the master bedroom suite and den. The public area consists of living room, kitchen and dining room. The guest wing offers privacy to visitors, and can be closed off by the owners when they are not entertaining.

Unexpected views of the Teton Mountain Range develop as one walks through the rooms. The entire story of the house is not told from the front; one needs to explore the spaces to uncover their special nature and to fully understand and appreciate their beauty and utility. This successful design supplies a structure, inside and out, to stimulate the inhabitants' senses.

Courtyards, patios and overhangs extend the liveability of the house and provide sheltered areas for entertaining amid this beautiful mountain setting. There has been a strong emphasis on architectural details in this new home, including square-cut tiles on the exterior of the fireplace and garden walls, a stacked stone fireplace, a cherry-veneered barrel vault ceiling and subtle cove lighting.

The mixture of rustic exterior with classical interior makes this remarkable home a real treasure.

1

Dubbe-Moulder Architects, PC

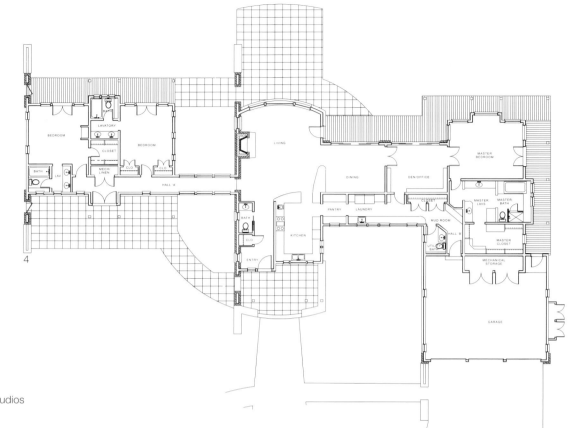

4 Single-level floor plan
5 Kitchen
6 Dining room
Photography: Woolly Bugger Studios

5

6

The House in Mani

Mani, Greece

Built in the late 19th century, this House in Mani, Greece, was originally a small, rectangular worker's cottage. The lower floor had been used to house animals while the upper floor consisted of three small rooms. A courtyard at the front of the house gave way to a lower level south-facing scrubland that sloped steeply and opened to views on all sides.

The owners live in the house four or five months a year, mainly in the summer. They had two main requirements: the first was to enlarge the built area to accommodate friends and visitors. The second was to create outdoor areas in which to relax and entertain in cool comfort at any time of day as the searing summer sun moved round the building.

1

The architects were involved on several levels: the landscaping of the garden, the building of a separate guest annexe in the courtyard and the addition of a stone-built bathroom and storage room. The wooden verandah lies between these two stone-built additions. A tiled roof over this space provides shade. The space created under it is now a paved terrace outside the main bedroom, ideal for breakfasts in summer.

Outdoor living in Greece is possible for nearly eight months of the year. Special care was taken to create functional and beautiful areas to maximise enjoyment of the garden. Designed on two levels, the garden takes advantage of the natural slope of the site and extensive views. Both these levels meet at either end with the garden orientated towards the south providing commanding views of the surroundings. The design merges the covered verandah and a freestanding bamboo-roofed pavilion.

The deliberately curved front wall of the guest annexe allows an easy visual flow from the gate to the stone well in the centre of the courtyard and beyond through a large arched entrance into the garden.

Special care was taken in the use of materials and construction techniques. Stone was selected from the local quarry – probably the source of the existing stone – continuing the trend of sourcing materials locally. Most cornerstones were purchased from derelict ruins in the country. A novel feature was the mixing of some garden soil to make the pointing exactly the same colour as the original, thus tying the new building in with the old.

Olive and almond trees that originally grew near the house were preserved if they were within the extension areas and incorporated within the structure where they continue to flourish.

Aiolou Architects

1   Terrace of main house leads down to courtyard shared with guest annexe
2   Guest annexe opens up to entrance courtyard that features stone well

3 View of south façade indicating all additions to original 19th-century cottage
4 Bedroom terrace offers sheltered relaxation throughout the day
5 Cosy nook provides respite from afternoon sun

3

4

5

6 Upper-level floor plan
7 Lower-level floor plan
8 Living room with traditional bamboo roof and original stone niches

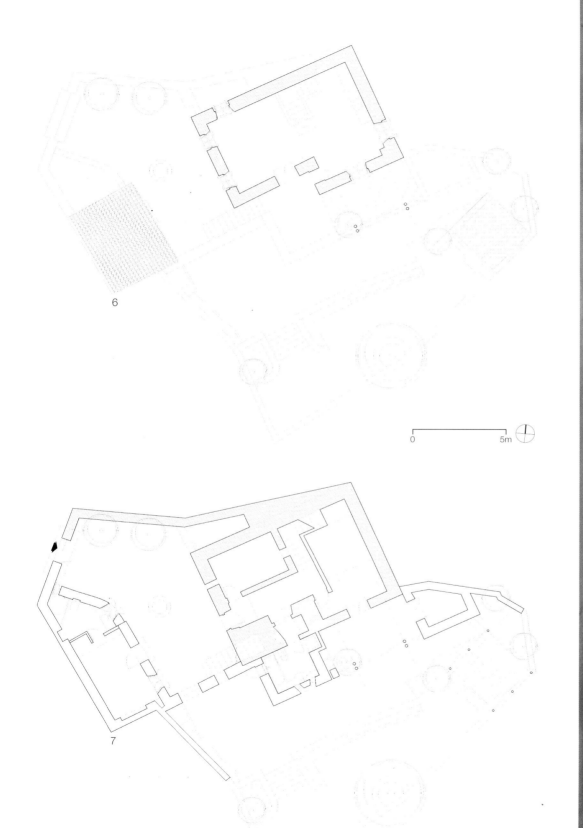

6

7

8

Opposite:
    Original external window transformed into interior feature of small bedroom
10 Solid sand-blasted marble counter maintains softness of natural materials
    used throughout house
11 New whitewashed concrete staircase with timber treads
Photography: Nikos Xanthopoulos

10

11

The Mill Creek House

Lake Hayes, New Zealand

The Mill Creek House is located on the edge of an old terraced bank overlooking Mill Creek. It is surrounded by the majestic mountain landscape of the Crown Range, Lake Hayes and Coronet Peak.

The site, a long narrow strip running from east to west, has panoramic views to both the south and west. On a lower level terrace, Mill Creek meanders across and feeds Lake Hayes. It provides transportation for freshwater brown trout during the breeding season from spawning ponds upstream. Once, rough pasture bordered the stream, but now the site has been developed into native wetlands with freshwater ponds where local birds and trout can breed.

The concept for the 350-square-metre vacation house took the form of a pavilion for relaxing and entertaining throughout the seasons. Guests could enjoy being totally immersed in the surrounding landscape.

A single-storey, L-shaped glazed pavilion opens to and surrounds a rectangular paved terrace orientated for both outdoor living and enjoying the western sunsets. The full-height glazed panes of the pavilion slide back, allowing the interior and exterior to merge across the upper paved terrace.

The upper terrace is complemented on one side by a large outdoor fireplace where family and guests can enjoy winter nights under the stars. On a lower terrace an outdoor kitchen facilitates preparation of summer meals.

The house is made up of an east–west orientated wing with sunken lounge, open-plan living area and kitchen and a north–south orientated wing consisting of the dining room, entry and guest suite on the lower level. This guest suite resembles a dark-stained, cedar-clad rectangular box orientated north–south and accommodates a large bunk room, bathroom, main bedroom suite and adjoining outdoor private terrace that floats over on the upper level.

The ceiling is a horizontal plane of cedar battens. Recycled *matai* timber flooring connected by glass panes focus the eye on the horizon, forming the lower level pavilion. Sunken into the main floor at the end of the east–west wing is a leather-lined conversation pit for relaxing while warmed by a big, open fire. Nearby cosy nooks for sitting and reading in the sun, frame the fireplace. Thick concrete-block walls form the outer walls of the 'L' and anchor the house to the site.

At dusk when the landscape disappears into muted darkness, the house takes on a lantern-like quality and appears almost suspended in its surroundings. It forms a welcoming beacon in the landscape.

1

1   House viewed from lower-level lawn
Opposite:
    Dusk view across terrace to living areas of pavilion

3 Dining area that opens out to terrace
4 Main bedroom looking towards private terrace
5 Conversation pit and fireplace
Photography: Dale Gardiner

3

4

5

The Nature House

Italian architect Fabrizio Ceccarelli has lived in Brazil for many years, and has developed a deep passion for the country. He was inspired for this project by the villages of indigenous people in the region, and has responded to their use of endemic, natural materials. Using their traditional design and building techniques he incorporated local wood, sisal rope ties, lime-painting and the use of branches to create this air-filled residence. The house is akin to the design of the Indian houses of the Xingu Reserve. An internal patio with a lovely garden surrounds all corners of the building.

The initial feeling upon entering the house is one of vast spaciousness. The interior garden acts as the core of the living areas incorporating the salon, living room and dining room. The four bedrooms appear to be hidden, underlining the tribal notion of protecting against aggressors.

The courtyard connects to the living areas across a bridge. It has a special view of the sea and the mountains, and conjures a sense of nature entering the home.

The colours and vibrant spirit of Brazil inspires the décor of this home with colourful walls, tiles and furniture. Internal rooms offer deep shade and a sun-splashed retreat from the heat of the day. Cool breezes flow through the house at night, and breaches in the roof provide glimpses of stars. The mountains, sea and gardens abound with tropical plants, heightening a sense of unity with nature.

1

1   Natural materials evoke a sense of oneness with nature
2   Bridge to master bedroom

Fabrizio Ceccarelli Arquiteto

5

7 Dining area
8 Stairway
9 Living room incorporating plants and sky
10 Detail of sisal rope ties
11 Roof detail
12 Opening in roof accommodates indoor plants
Photography: Sergio Pagano

7

8

9

10

11

12

The Price Residence

Washington D.C., USA

The simple and natural virtues of the site's trees and rocky outcrops inspired the design of this residence. An abundance of trees splitting rocks over a streambed is the essence of the park that runs through the centre of Washington D.C. Likewise this home, sited in that park, is dedicated to trees that eat the rocks. Floating amid the old soul trees, quietly in tune with the seasons, it sits boldly present.

The home is seen as an abstracted tree. On the street side it is clad in patina copper and suspended on two columns, hung by steel cables, at the cliff's edge. The park side rear is clad with transparent super-insulated glazing. The sides are translucent fibreglass panels for privacy and soft transitional light. Major trees have been saved and continue their upward path through the house.

The home sits high up on a 30-metre cliff edge, appearing to soar out over a perennial stream. This stream feeds Rock Creek and eventually the mighty Potomac River. Its four floors are wrapped in patina copper and glass with two trunk-like columns of steel. The design attempts to blend into the park by mimicking its colours, while its use of glass reflects the surrounding trees. Curving walls echo the never-ending paths of nature.

The approach to the residence is over a glass bridge and entry is through a small glass portal cut into a large green mass of copper. Crossing the glass bridge suspends time and delivers a sense of elevation from the earth. Wood is a dominant feature expressed in maple walls and Brazilian cherry wood floors. Steel, glass and wood complete the full authenticity of the design.

The top floor is a master bedroom with glass on all four sides surrounded by a rooftop garden. Nature's elements: the changing of seasons, trees, the sun, moon and stars are all in full view.

Stillness, movement and nature, the three lenses for enduring architecture are evident in the home's design with trees, sunlight and gravity portraying nature. Stillness is reflected in its suspended Zen simplicity. Movement is the power of explosive views riding the dynamic forces of gravity in defiance. The dynamic movement of never-ending space blends with a meditative minimalism and natural drama. Warmth and openness blend seamlessly in this modernist home, at once a tree and yet an urban loft.

1

Travis Price Architects

3   Media room on lowest level
4   Master bedroom with large glazed areas
5   Stainless steel kitchen bench and glass-encased
    spiral stair
Opposite:
    Living room with study loft above. Steel rods hold
    entire house
Photography: Ken Wyner

3

4

5

The Quogue Residence

Long Island, New York, USA

This residence is located in Quogue, New York – a summer residential community of early 20th-century shingle-style houses. Originally, the site included a small rundown house at the back of the long, flat, rectangular site which was overgrown at the front. By demolishing the dilapidated house and clearing the overgrowth, the site proved both sunny and private. The new house was set forward on this site creating an expansive back yard with ample room for gardens, a pool and pool house.

As the summer home for a family with young children, the clients sought a design that would easily accommodate and entertain their frequent visitors, and offer access to the outside gardens and pool. Bedrooms for guests and children were necessary, but the clients did not want a large, rambling house. At approximately 613 square metres, this house includes five bedrooms, with a sixth guest bedroom in the tower.

The large wrap-around porch at the rear connects to the family room, kitchen and living room. This provides an open summer connection between the outside and inside. A screen porch with a fireplace can be transformed to a warmer room by installing windows for autumn and spring evenings. The front porch opens to a formal entrance on the right and informal entrance to the large mudroom on the left.

The kitchen and adjoining family room overlook the back yard and pool area, forming the central gathering area of the house. The spacious kitchen includes a custom-made breakfast area and an eat-in counter with bar stools. All counter tops are cherry wood with the exception of sections next to the sink which are of green slate.

The clients' desire was a shingle-style house reminiscent but not duplicating the early 20th-century houses of the area. It was designed and crafted with numerous details that set it as a 21st-century shingle-style structure, yet it retains an elegant sense of the past. With a brick base, the Alaskan yellow-cedar shingled house includes wood mullion windows, a fir floor and cherry for the kitchen counter tops, panelled library, staircase cap and rail. Full of cosy nooks this residence is a warm and enchanting retreat.

1

Austin Patterson Disston Architects LLC

1   Library is set in octagonal section of house
2   Front exterior – gambrel roof, porches, diamond-paned windows, columns
    and octagonal room refer to traditional shingle-style homes in the area

2

3 Ground-floor plan
4 Second-floor plan
5 Beadboard walls, custom cabinets, slate and cherry countertops and a multi-purpose island make up the kitchen

6 Breaking up kitchen space, a breakfast nook was tucked into window bay
7 Upper stairway; arched beadboard ceiling and mahogany mouldings are features of second-floor landing
8 Located adjacent to the kitchen, the family room provides a double-height space with wide beadboard trim, transom windows and slate fireplace

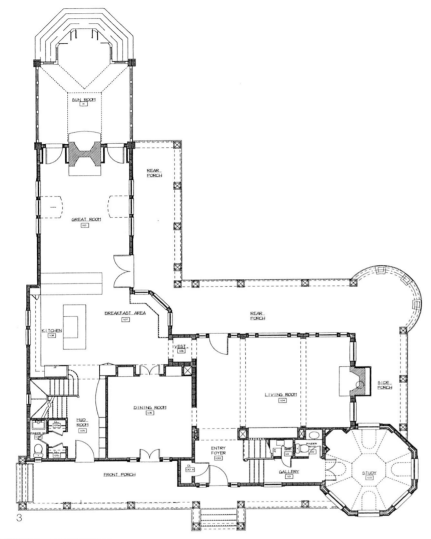

3

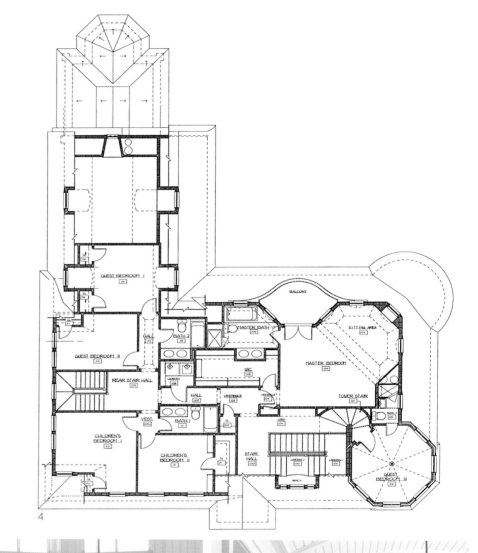

4

5

6

7

9 Rear exterior – gambrel roof includes a rap porch and upper balcony porch off master bedroom
10 Living room has transom windows with diamond inserts that bring down the sight line of the room
    and add more sight. Black slate and glass-tile fireplace surround lends modern touch
Photography: Jeff McNamara

10

The Stone Residence

Oconee County,
South Carolina, USA

The Stone Residence at the Seven Acre Point is located on the edge of a designated area of outstanding natural beauty on scenic Lake Hartwell in upstate South Carolina. The land is densely wooded with pine and oak trees, and surrounded on three sides by the lake. A gravel road through the woods leads to the house.

This shingle-style house was designed to provide a weekend retreat for relaxation, allowing time to gaze out at the magnificent lake views. The house was sensitively integrated into the landscape and maximises views across the lake.

The house has more than 465 square metres of indoor space and almost 186 square metres of exterior porches. Once in the entry porch, the view unfolds first to the living room and then out to the screen porch, finally taking in Lake Hartwell. The stone fireplace in the living room is located on axis with the dining room and wraparound screen porch. Almost all the rooms on the first floor and the attic floor have a lake view. The attic floor houses guest bedrooms, the games room, a private office and a loft that overlooks the living room. An open wood staircase provides access between the two floors.

The design minimises solar heat gain by orientating the house along an east–west axis. This orientation also catches the prevailing wind and enhances the benefits of natural ventilation. Cross ventilation is provided by more than 70 windows and strategically located exterior doors.

The house lends itself to the enjoyment of the sensitive landscaping of the grounds, and links to the natural environment. The landscape plant palette is composed of materials that are compatible with surrounding indigenous plants. The design incorporates natural materials: Tennessee fieldstone for the porch columns and fireplace, and cedar shingles for the house. Local craftsmen knowledgeable in traditional construction techniques were employed to carry out the work. This home is both cosy and inviting.

1

1   View of house through woods
2   View of house facing lake

Joseph Michael Kelly, Architect

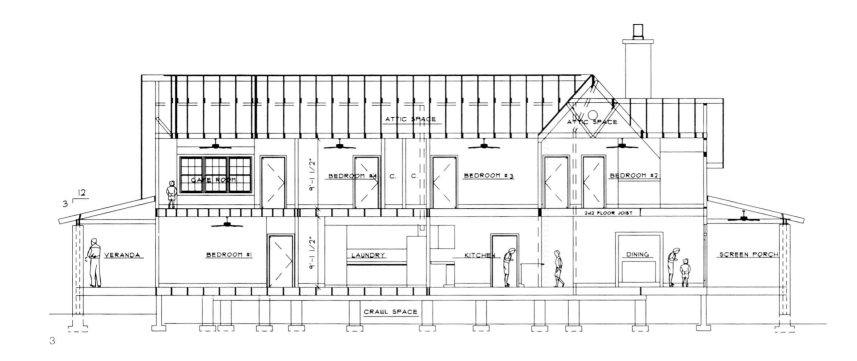

3

4

5

The Turtle House

Manasota Key, Sarasota, Florida, USA

The clients' original brief called for a retirement beach house in traditional mode. The presence of a Harley-Davidson motorcycle in the living room and numerous other clues suggested a less conventional lifestyle. The idea of a 'turtle house' emerged from studies of the island of Manasota Key, a haven for the endangered sea turtle.

The weather conditions of the site required the project to respond to extremes of searing sun and hurricane storms. The building needed to be designed to withstand high winds with water surges. For this purpose, the structure is grounded on concrete piles extending into the earth as deep as the building is tall. Twelve doors provide ready access to shaded porches surrounding all floors on three sides. The porches allow enjoyment of the tranquil environment and avoid the relentless heat and glare. Another climatic attribute in this region of the USA is torrential rainfall. Well-concealed continuous slots at the roof edges collect the rain. The supporting functions of the building – the stairs and elevator – are organised at the north side of the square plan. This strategy allows the living spaces to take advantage of the lovely sunrises and sunsets and overlook the island to the south.

The primary structure for this beautifully symmetrical residence is of cast-in-place concrete columns and slabs supported by driven pre-cast concrete piles. Cantilever slabs form the deck areas. The roof structure is wood-framed with a central arched concrete girder. The exterior finish is unpainted plaster and the roof is painted steel.

The environment has been factored into the design of this beach house. Separate packaged heat-pump systems, one system for the lower floor and one for the upper two floors, provide heating and cooling. Glazing is low E–insulated glass coated to reduce solar heat gain. The location of the site close to a turtle hatching zone necessitates shielding off light coming from the house to prevent turtle hatchlings mistaking it for moonlight. Moonlight provides the means by which hatchlings find their way to the sea. By limiting the light emitted from the house, the hatchlings are more likely to be attracted down to the beach, and from there begin their journey into the gulf waters and out to sea.

The overhangs provide shade and create outdoor spaces at the upper floors to enjoy breezes and views from the gulf and bay side. Open planning provides natural light, encourages the use of cross-ventilation and promotes indoor/outdoor living year round.

Viewed from the Gulf of Mexico side, the house appears nestled in a natural dune. This provides a measure of protection for the structure from the extremes of weather. The curved shape of the roof and the safe, protective space inside are reminiscent of a turtle shell. Fixed lighting mimics the shape of turtle eggs. All these design features emphasise the importance of the built environment working sensitively with the natural environment.

1

1 Viewed from Gulf of Mexico, home is nestled in natural sand dunes
Opposite:
    Refined, symbolic metaphor of turtle as shelter

Previous pages:
  Curved interior wall separates circulation space
  from open living space
4 Large glazed areas offer views to water and
   natural landscape that surrounds home
5 Reflected views of Gulf of Mexico in master
   bathroom adds to transparency of home
6 Large kitchen with absolute black granite
   countertops and maple cabinets emphasise
   restraint in architecture
Photography: George Cott

5

6

Vacation Estate

Florida, USA

From the road, this Florida vacation residence is solid and private. From the inside it is totally open to the Gulf of Mexico. The form-giver is the triangular-shaped site, with dramatic views to the Gulf. Light, the sun angles and shadows, the breezes and the tropical landscape are all major factors taken into account with this design.

The half-hectare site is triangular. The design concept is formed of two rectangles and a tall *brise soleil* (grand loggia). The rectangles are set at angles to capture sweeping views up and down the beach. The *brise soleil* acts as the organising element. The restrictive state coastal codes have been turned into assets, adding views across 300 metres of unbuildable adjacent beach frontages.

The house is grand in scale and is designed as though the site extended to the horizon. It has high ceilings, tall columns and expansive glass walls. This is a pavilion of six inter-related levels open to the view. The living space is on the main level, bedrooms above and guest-suite and playroom below. The terrace that visually reaches out to the water is accessed via a bridge.

The building is a structural presence informed by the site, which through these gestures of movement and reach becomes part of the environment.

1 Main entry
2 Main house – view from beach

Carl Abbott FAIA, Architects/Planners PA

3 Second-floor plan
4 First-floor plan
5 Pool terrace with main house to right. Bridge and terrace of guest suite is
  to left with view to Gulf of Mexico
6 View to pool terrace; main house to left and guest suite to right

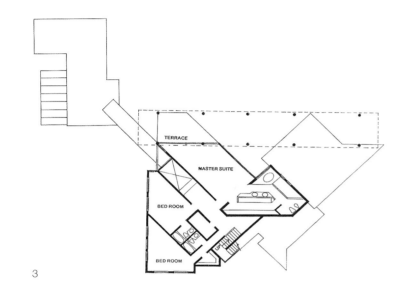

3

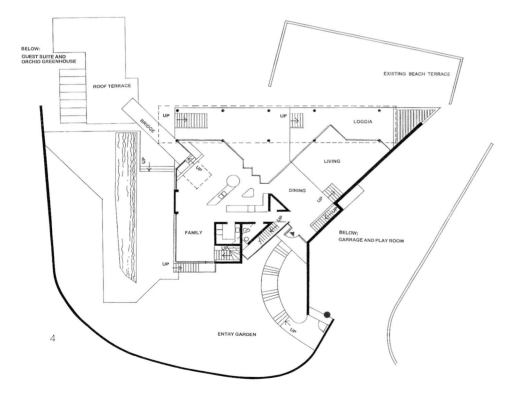

4

5

6

7

7   Living/dining space with sweeping views out to Gulf of Mexico
8   View to Gulf from upper level study
9   Master suite with view to Gulf
Photography: ©Steven Brooke Studio

8

9

Valhalla

Located on the outskirts of Iceland's capital, Reykjavic, this summer residence rises in the distance looking somewhat like a medieval castle. Located in the untouched hinterland of Iceland's capital, Reykjavic, the residence is inextricably bonded to its site. On the 30-minute drive from the capital, a turn in the road reveals sweeping views over a long, lake-filled valley. The residence overlooks Thingvallavtn Lake, and is within walking distance of the world's first parliament site. It is a landscape of international significance and is anticipated to soon become a UNESCO world heritage site.

The surrounding fractured lava surface of the ground is coated in a thin film of moss, lichen and other minimal vegetation. Throughout the seasons this vegetation changes colour almost imperceptibly, an effect magnified by the scale and remoteness of the setting. In this extraordinary context, the twisted form of the house half hovers and half perches, not unlike the broken rock of which the site is formed.

The house is approached on foot via a path of handpicked lava plate. This route follows the line of the land and the gnarled birch growth surrounding the entrance to the house obscures the view. The view hidden by the approach unfolds slowly. A small lobby opens into the living room door, where the magnificent snow-capped mountain Skjaldbreid appears framed by the huge picture window. A turn to the right and a panorama of Thingvallavtn Lake fills the room, drawing one out to the terrace to see clouds of geothermal steam drifting over the southern mountain ridge.

On first impression, this would appear to constitute just a house, but the plan is deceiving. New spaces and another wing reveal themselves as the inner areas of the house are explored. Tucked into a corner, with its own lake view, is the kitchen bedecked in the bright yellow and red hues of autumn moss. At the opposite corner, an iroko stairway leads down to the lower library, study and bedroom wing. Each of the rooms has full-height doors, ideal to throw open on sunny mornings. The deep-water coloured master bedroom has a balcony cantilevering out towards the lake.

These subtle spatial relationships are wrapped in a delicate skin of weathered fir boarding with a roof of lichen and rock that will, in time, gather a patina to become indistinguishable from the virgin site. The design seeks to enhance the qualities of remoteness and timelessness that makes this place so attractive. Consideration has been given to the impact that human occupation has on this site, and the design seeks to limit, while minimising any damage the residence will bequeath to the surrounding environment.

1

Studio Granda

2

3

Opposite:
    Fireplace and seat with framed view of symmetrical mountain Skjaldbreid
5   Library steps
6   Window behind fireplace to catch glow of setting sun
7   Bedroom wing corridor leading to library steps and study
Photography: Sigurgeir Sigurjónsson

5

6

7

Villa Nilsson

Varberg, Sweden

The architect's intent was to design a very simple house that from the outside looks unpretentious. The understated façade gives no indication of the spectacular and uninterrupted view of the ocean that unfolds once within, or the spacious sunlit feel of the interior.

Large, sliding glass doors provide ample access to the terraces. Glass canopies provide shade from the sun through delicately cut team planks with an aerofoil section supported by a cantilevered beam.

The rock within the site penetrates the floor and the wall becomes part of the interior. The inner wall, parallel to the view is top-lit by a skylight catching the sun as it travels from east to west and casts shadows of the protruding beams.

As illustrated by Ruskin in the *Stones of Venice*, ageing is an important aspect of life, art and architecture. The design for this villa considers this element: in time, the entire villa will assume a grey patina of age. The untreated aluminium in the roof will corrode and take on a dark stain; the untreated teak will become a light grey colour and pieces of the comb-cut aerofoiled sunshades will gradually lose their teeth as the wood cracks, creating a subtle, picturesque silhouette of change.

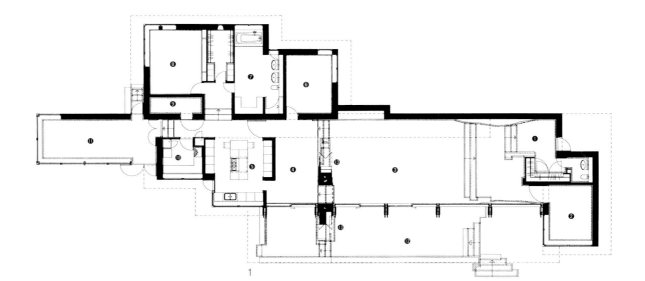

1

Wingardh & Wingardh AB

3   Looking southwest along terrace
4   Living area viewed from dining room
Following pages:
    Northwest elevation from coastline
Photography: Tim Griffith

3

4

Villa Bled

Villa Bled is an extension of a 19th-century villa located in the beautiful Lake Bled alpine resort. The client's major requirement was that most spaces have views towards the lake. The client also required that the size of the main living area be twice the size of the old villa. Since both the old villa and the landscape were heritage listed, the main task was to incorporate the new 700-square-metre addition within the restrictions that bound the villa and the surrounding landscape.

New spaces created under the ground floor of the existing villa and the extension surrounding it form a circular base around the house: a 'pillow' sitting comfortably within the landscape. This pillow, when viewed from the other side of the lake, blends with the hilly surroundings. The area under the pillow is glazed and overlooks the lake. Floor levels are varying and follow the undulating terrain. These levels are used to create different rooms and spaces. The roof of the new pillow becomes a terrace and garden in front of the upper floor, where the children's area is located.

Living spaces such as the informal kitchen, dining and television areas are enhanced by a fireplace and audio facilities. The library and working spaces are located along the glazed façade of the ground floor. The restroom, closets, main kitchen and laundry are hidden behind the walls of the old villa that penetrate from above. The two upper floors of the old villa comprise family and private areas; primarily for the children and parents.

From the entrance porch, the view is opened through the main axis of the house. Views of the lake dominate through the sweeping spiral staircase. The entrance of the main house is deliberately disengaged from this axis, compelling entry from the side. Once inside, one crosses a water feature and passes under the staircase hall. Looking upward, the spaces of the old villa open in a gallery-style space. The curved stairway connects the new and old parts of the house and all the main areas are open to the stairway and main lobby.

The new extension is glazed. The pillow around the terrace, forming a fence and providing shade, is made of wood. Wood, which is a traditional material in alpine areas, is also used for cladding interior spaces. Wood floors, walls and ceilings combine with other materials such as ceramic in the bathrooms, leather in closets, and glass and mirrors in the kitchen. All wardrobes and doors to private rooms are in the same material as the wall cladding and blend seamlessly together.

1

Ofis Arhitekti

4

5 'Her' bathroom
6 Entry to living room under spiral stairway
7 Entrance courtyard
8 Horizontal axis towards entry
Photography: Tomaz Gregoric

5

6

7

8

Walski Residence

Emerging out of a rocky narrow ledge of the desert slope, the structure of this well-protected home seems to expand into the surrounding landscape. The design merges form, texture and environment to become one harmonious whole. The architect drew on tangible and intangible sources of inspiration to fashion this home to suit the client's lifestyle.

Entry from the street is gained through an arch-shaped, stone-clad wall. Just inside, another curved wall is juxtaposed by a steel gate that penetrates the wall and reaches all the way to the ground. The entry gate has water flowing on both surfaces of rippled glass and opens to a large courtyard with a reflecting pool. Water plays a major role as a feature in this house contrasting with the arid environment.

1

On the second floor, the separate guesthouse is as engaging as the master suite. It has a wet bar, entertainment centre, a large private terrace and view to the fairway. The major entertainment area, family room, morning room and master suites are designed to have a seamless connection between the indoors and outdoors. When all the pocket doors are open, the house seems to recede into the background as the sculptural desert landscape comes into focus.

The image of a tropical oasis was strengthened by some surprising natural elements brought inside. The reflecting pool first encountered in the courtyard, continues inside the house. The bold, geometric forms cut out of the floor highlight and emphasise water which is, especially in an arid climate, a sacred commodity.

The formal dining room is cantilevered over the reflecting pool with glass doors that disappear into pockets. The master suite is both private and elegant, with large closets. It also has separate baths, a sitting area, an office and space for art niches and displays.

Tall, vaulted wood-panelled ceilings are featured in the entertaining area. Custom-built fireplaces add warmth and intimacy on those cold desert nights, and cove lighting subtly illuminates throughout. A circular, sunken bar is fully equipped with refrigerator and icemaker, while the kitchen is fitted with state-of-the-art appliances and a cable-suspended hood.

Using the principles of sustainable design, this home was designed with the environment in mind. The architect's goal was to create a building that is environmentally responsible and a healthy, relaxing, aesthetic place to live.

Patel Architecture/Narendra Patel, AIA

1   Waterfall from roof into seemingly overflowing pool adds whimsical touch to outdoor areas
2   Dining room cantilevered over reflecting pool. Disappearing glass projects the feel of dining
    room floating on water
Following pages:
    Boundary between indoors and outdoors is erased by incorporating motorised trackless
    glass doors that disappear with the touch of a button

4 Indoors and outdoors seamlessly blend together
5 Powder room
6 Sensual serpentine ceiling, multi-layered headboard
  and luxurious bed form key accents of master suite
Photography: David Glomb

5

4

Weekend House at Bhati Mines

Bhati Mines, Aravalli Range, India

This home, on the outskirts of the capital Delhi, is an ode to the colours and vibrancy of the desert state of Rajasthan, in northwest India. The owners wanted a two-bedroom residence on a six-hectare farm in the Aravalli Hills. They envisaged the house surrounded by fruit orchards and lush gardens. The site in the Bhati mines area is arid and rocky with a few small hills.

Many factors inspired the architect. The elaborate design draws on local architectural style and construction methods. Mud and only a small amount of wood is used to recreate this style, and the walls are decorated with the elaborately painted wall frescoes for which Rajasthan is famous. Rajasthani tradition is thus combined with modern amenities to ensure comfort. This rustic and private farmhouse serves as a weekend retreat for contemplation, solitude and occasional entertaining.

A rustic and uneven finish was achieved for the façade using traditional construction methods and contouring bricks for a mud plaster effect. The design presents uncluttered spaciousness as living spaces merge with each other. Yellow Jaisalmer and black Cuddapah stone flooring impart a warm and earthy glow. Auspicious symbols like the *sriyantra* motif (symbolic of the goddess of wealth) at the entrance provide interest.

Upon entering, a sense of spaciousness is observed, created by the skilful delineation of the open plan. A stepped divider between the living, lounge, dining and open kitchen areas with a small partition across both sides of the main door create physical, not visual barriers.

A sense of calm is prevalent upon entering the long rectangular hall, which is covered with bright *bandhani* (tie and dyed) silk fabric interwoven with gold ribbon. Cushions of different shapes, colours and sizes, embroidered with sequins and mirrors are scattered around.

The rooms are in visual contact with the Jaipur blue-tiled swimming pool in the middle of the farm. Coloured glass on doors, windows, and built-in light fixtures is a dominant feature throughout the house. The beds, seating areas, tables and low-height Indian-style seating near the fireplace are all from masonry.

The centrally located pool cools the interiors naturally, and the water is recycled for irrigation. The five elements of *vaastu*: air, water, sky, fire and earth are integrated into the design of the house. Textures and shapes play a prominent and decorative role.

1

Praachi Design Pvt. Ltd.

1 Jaipur blue-tiled swimming pool in centre of house is ideal for poolside parties
2 Façade represents the *haveli** style of architecture
3 Dining area next to open kitchen with wrought-iron table, probably the only visible modern accent
4 Built-in beds, ethnic furniture and accessories enhance traditional spirit of place

5 One of two bedrooms, with brightly coloured glass on openings flanked by coloured lights
Photography: Taj Mohammed

*A term that refers to a personal residence in the Shekhawati and Marwar regions of India.
The word *haveli* is of Persian origin meaning 'enclosed space'.

2

3   4   5

Winter House

An Island in the Gulf of Mexico

This beach house is a series of light terraces which appear to float in a canopy of trees. Running the full height of the structure, a vertical space visually anchors the terraces to the tropical site.

The architectural brief was for a winter house that was exhilarating to live in, evoking a feeling of lightness. It was to be open to sun, sky and the turquoise waters of the Gulf of Mexico.

Responding to the tropical climate, this house is located on the beach of a Gulf-front island. The narrow, heavily wooded site is surrounded by large condominium structures.

The design of the house has grown from the dominant surrounding conditions and the need to capture the views of the beach and Gulf. One terrace thrusts out towards the west, facing the winter sunsets. The other terrace reaches out to the southwest end of the crescent-shaped beach. Affecting the form of this design are the neighbouring structures – houses on the same site and the large condominiums on adjacent properties. The existing trees, sun angles and winds were all factors in determining the final form of this house.

Throughout, materials have been chosen that weather well and blend with the environment – bleached silver-grey wood, Mexican tile and clear glass. The site's trees, beach, water and sky are all incorporated as materials of the building. The curved contours of the house resonate with the flow of waves, the imprint of water on pristine beaches and the curl of clouds. The house evokes a sense of being an extension of the site itself.

1

1   From upper terrace looking down to first-level terrace
Opposite:
    Upper-level living room with view to Gulf of Mexico

Carl Abbott FAIA Architects/Planners PA

4

5   First-level living/dining area with view to terrace and Gulf beyond
6   Upper-level living room

6

7　View from dining area to vertical stairway
Opposite:
　First-level living area with vertical stairway and view to Gulf
Photography: ©Steven Brooke Studios

7

Yautepec House

1

Sited an hour-and-a-half from Mexico City in a farming community, the land has been reclaimed from an acre of cornfields. The climatic conditions are extreme, with hot, dry winters and warm, rainy summers. An experimental approach was taken by the architect to arrive at the best design to meet the challenges this home presented.

The house is designed with specific consideration for the landscape, with the view towards the Tepozteco Mountains taken into account. Shady areas have been created using pergolas; and a wide variety of plants and trees with different microclimate needs are grown here.

Architecturally, the building is composed of separate building wings, one more open than the other. The more open wing contains common areas such as a living room, dining room and kitchen. The other contains the bedrooms and bathrooms. The design was conceived, using natural surroundings as an extension of enclosed spaces, to encourage the occupants to change atmospheres as they moved around the dwelling. A broad bower, covered by vines, provides protection against light and heat for both buildings.

The landscape surrounding the buildings was a conditioning factor for the design of the garden, with the characteristic climate of the site taken into account. More than a hundred different species of orchids, as well as zapote, banana, tamarind, papaya and guava trees constitute the great variety of vegetation. Many other design elements make up the final integral form of the park. These include sequence, spontaneity and organic forms The overall objective was that this garden not appear prefabricated, but that it expresses a very personal point of view of nature.

1 Landscaped gardens with exotic tree and plant varieties
2 Site plan shows two wings
3 Separate wings converge on gardens
4 Broad, vine-covered bower protects walkway from light and heat
5 Water features add a feel of coolness
6 Portion of garden
7 Interior wing with living spaces is airy and spacious
Photography: Alberto Moreno

Index

Acknowledgments

IMAGES acknowledges the invaluable contribution of the many architects whose work appears within the pages of this book. Without their willingness and enthusiasm, this publication would not be a reality.

We also acknowledge the role of the many photographers whose wonderful visual imagery helped, in no small measure, transport readers to their 'perfect getaway'.

Photography credits on Page 8:
Aarthun Residence – Nicola Pira
House in Mani – Nikos Xanthopoulos
Villa Bled – Tomaz Gregoric
The Nature House – Sergio Pagano

Every effort has been made to trace the original source of copyright material contained in this book. The publishers would be pleased to hear from copyright holders to rectify any errors or omissions. The information and illustrations in this publication have been prepared and supplied by the entrants. While all reasonable efforts have been made to source the required information and ensure accuracy, the publishers do not, under any circumstances, accept responsibility for errors, omissions and representations express or implied.